THE PERFECT GIFT

The birth of Jesus – the turning point of history

THE PERFECT GIFT

The birth of Jesus – the turning point of history

PHILIP GREENSLADE

Published by CWR, Waverley Abbey House, Waverley Lane, Farnham, Surrey GU9 8EP England.

Concept development, editing, design and production by CWR.
Printed in Finland by WS Bookwell.

ISBN 1-85345-246-7

CONTENTS

FOREWORD

I well remember, as a young visiting preacher still at Bible college, causing consternation to many a church organist by selecting 'Hark the herald angels sing' as the opening hymn in the middle of June. Like many, I relish the rhythm of the Christian Year. Its regular feasts and festivals mirror the involvement of God in actual history and the Son of God's immersion in our human condition. But since He is the 'man for all seasons' I trust these reflections will be read with profit at any time of the year.

This small book – like Jesus Himself – is for life, not just for Christmas!

These meditations also assume that we might conceivably be sometimes more concerned with God and what He is doing than preoccupied with the 'mumps and measles' of our own souls. It is admittedly a big assumption. Martyn Lloyd-Jones' sober assessment may well still ring true.

> I verily believe that the main trouble of most evangelical people today is that they read their Bibles too devotionally, which means, I say, subjectively. And this mighty panorama of the acts of the living God is something we seem to be unaware of and the result is that we need to be reminded of what God has done. (*Revival*, p.96)

In saying this, Dr Lloyd-Jones admitted he might be misunderstood. Certainly we should beware of an *un*devotional theology that appeals only to arcane and cerebral interests. But his point is well taken. Perhaps it's not too much to hope that we might celebrate the mighty deeds of God in history with our minds wonderingly stretched *and*, at the same time, feel them stirring our 'spiritual blood' and warming our hearts.

These reflections have been shared at various times and with various congregations, not least with the keen hearers with whom I enjoyed such stimulating fellowship on a series of Bible study evenings at Waverley Abbey House in Farnham. I hope those who kindly encouraged their reproduction in print, particularly John Peters, may find some satisfaction in the outcome. The focus was then as it is here on the infancy narratives as told by Matthew and Luke, but I have topped and tailed them with a word from Paul and John.

It will be only too obvious that these reflections are suggestive rather than definitive, chiefly because in reflecting on the nativity stories we are gazing on a great and unfathomable wonder. So these pieces, in the words of the book of Job, touch only the 'outskirts of God's ways'. Repetition is inevitable as we turn the 'diamond' this way and that to catch another glimmer of reflected light.

I am again in debt to my good friend Trevor Martin, who did much early editorial work on this book, to the skilled design and editorial team at CWR, and to my wife, Mary, who as usual was a discerning proofreader and dialogue partner.

Much of my recent work has been sponsored and encouraged by CWR, and its founder, my friend,

Selwyn Hughes, whose passion for the gospel I share and whose generosity of spirit allows us to be different. I dedicate this book to him with sincere respect and genuine affection.

PREVIEW

Perfect Timing

> But when *the fullness of time had come*, God sent forth his Son, born of woman, born under the law, to redeem those who were under the law, so that we might receive adoption as sons. And because you are sons, God has sent the Spirit of his Son into our hearts, crying, 'Abba! Father!' So you are no longer a slave, but a son, and if a son, then an heir through God.
>
> Gal. 4:4–7, ESV, my italics

The passing of time fascinates us and frustrates us. In Terry Pratchett's Discworld fantasy, *Thief of Time*, a secret group called 'the monks of history' hoard all the time that's ever been wasted in the world and pipe it to those who need more time. We wish!

'How *time flies* ...' we bemoan, as if we should be any more surprised than a fish is surprised by the wetness of water. We are temporal creatures; time is our natural habitat.

Time will heal, we trust, after suffering pain, but it usually leaves a psychological scar concealing an old wound, covering over a piece of emotional shrapnel embedded in our war-torn memory.

Time will tell, we say, hoping that history will judge us favourably, that the future will vindicate us, that our own epitaph will be worth the price of the headstone. But it is not always so; the wicked still prosper and the good still die young.

Above all, we complain of the *tyranny of time*. Horace Whitell, a British dockworker from Gillingham in Kent, hated his alarm clock. Every day for forty-seven years its strident bell jarred him awake, and for forty-seven years he longed to ignore it. Finally Horace got his revenge. On the day he retired, Mr Whitell flattened the alarm clock under an 80-ton hydraulic press. 'It was,' he said, 'a lovely feeling.'

Such feelings are a fleeting respite from what we perceive to be the mundane round of activities. At best this can be a comforting routine; at worst, the cyclic repetition, which the preacher of Ecclesiastes felt, too often seems to add up to nothing but mere meaninglessness.

The poet Dylan Thomas reflected ruefully on the unpitying passage of time since his carefree 'lamb-white' days:

> Oh as I was young and easy in the mercy of his means
> Time held me, green and dying
> Though I sang in my chains like the sea.[1]

Only God gives time meaning.

> But when *the fullness of time had come*, God sent forth his Son, born of woman, born under the law, to redeem those who were under the law, so that we might receive adoption as sons.
>
> Gal. 4:4, ESV, my italics

God's time is 'the fullness of time'. The phrase suggests the image of a container slowly filling up to its limit. God's time is not primarily, if at all, to do with the way the world is ordering its affairs. Preachers once rhapsodised over the way in which the *Pax Romana* and Roman roads and law made conditions suitable for the spread of the gospel. But this is not Paul's concern. His focus is on the arrival of the 'date set by the father' (Gal. 4:2, ESV) for his sons to inherit his estate. Until such a time comes, these sons are in one sense no more advantaged than slaves in the father's household. But now their time of inheritance has arrived. Similarly the time has now come for God's once-born sons to inherit the full blessings of salvation .

The 'until' that leads up to God's appointed time is now complete; the crucial phase of his redemptive purpose can now be worked out.

It used to be said that the biblical view of time was distinctive in the ancient world in being linear, not cyclical. This is too stark a distinction. After all, the Old Testament life of Israel was governed by the regular rhythm of repeated weekly, monthly and annual feasts. Better to say that time in biblical terms is coherent and cumulative, progressive and eschatological.

It presupposes that history is real and going somewhere, that it has a beginning, a middle and an end. And above all it celebrates that the world's 'times are in his hands'. History, as they say, is His-story.

God's age-old purposes have now reached their climax, says Paul. There was a 'before'; there is now an 'after' – BC and AD (to use what are now politically incorrect tabs).

In the words of the leading Christian historian, Jaroslav Pelikan,

> Eventually the very calendar of Europe – which then became the calendar for most of the world – evolved into a recognition of ... the significance of the figure of Jesus

> as the turning point of history, turning point of history as process and of history as narrative.[2]

The fullness of time has already arrived. No evolutionary process is needed to explain this. The Last Days have begun. The turning-point of history has already occurred. Synchronise with God's time or miss out completely.

The filling-up of God's purpose has overflowed in the sending of the Son. Being 'born of a woman', Jesus shared our humanness, our common humanity; being 'born under Torah' He shared Jewish humanness; He was a Jew committed to doing God's will as He lived out the story of God's people.

He was sent to us this way 'in order to redeem those under the law'. In other words, His first mission was to release Israel from bondage and into the full-grown sonship for which its history and destiny had prepared it. And He aimed to achieve this 'so that we might receive adoption as sons' – that is all of us, Jews and Gentiles. His ultimate mission was to recover for the fallen sons of Adam their lost status as the sons of God.

The movement of the Son would, in due course, be matched by the movement of the Holy Spirit.

> And because you are sons, God has sent the Spirit of his Son into our hearts, crying, 'Abba! Father!' So you are no longer a slave, but a son, and if a son, then an heir through God .
>
> Gal. 4:6–7, ESV

The sending of the Spirit of the Son is 'into our hearts', so that this is no merely legal adoption but a heart-felt experience. The Spirit is here rightly called the 'Spirit of his Son' so that the one Spirit of God, the Spirit active in creation and life and prophecy, now comes to us stamped with the character of Jesus.

The fullness of time is a challenge to all of us to synchronise our time with God's by faith. The fullness of time is an intensely concentrated focus on the sending of the Son. C.S. Lewis called it 'the Grand Miracle'. For journalist Malcolm Muggeridge, buffeted by doubts, it was a cable-bridge, swaying but reliable, which connected him to God. Karl Barth called it 'the great "Yes"'. For the apostle John, it was the uttering of God's final word. For Paul elsewhere it was simply God's 'unspeakable gift'.

It is a prophetic idea whose time has come. 'It' is the incarnation – the taking flesh of the eternal Son of God, Whom we know as Jesus. Matthew and Luke tell the story of His birth in Bethlehem as the story of God's perfect gift, Jesus, come in God's perfect time.

CHAPTER ONE

Great Preparations – Matthew's Viewpoint

Read Matthew 1–2

Dust-covered files, dog-eared legal documents, yellowing birth certificates. It seems an unpromising beginning to what we've been led to believe is the greatest story ever told. It seems to confirm the impression that our message is about ancient history locked up in long-forgotten scrolls. Matthew, whom we had assumed was the evangelist of good news, seems to be diverting us into taking a trip down memory lane to visit some long-neglected records office, there to rummage about in musty archives. He offers us a *genealogy*.

To rootless, early twenty-first-century Western minds, it feels like cultural archaeology, just a boring list of names, but to a first-century Jew it was a dramatic family tree – because it was *his* family tree.

Matthew, who worked in a tax office, may have had a particular relish for lists, columns and old receipts. But a stereotypical, civil-service mind-set does not explain why he starts his Gospel this way. He has a larger reason in mind, which at one level is plain enough: important events take long-term planning. With the coming of Jesus Christ surface the best-laid plans of the one Creator God. His advent is the culmination of God's long-term strategy, the fruition of a far-off story that began with Abraham (Matt. 1:1), the founding father of faith who stepped out of comfortable retirement into a huge adventure with his God.

The birth of Jesus therefore represents the final, conclusive chapter of the old stories written about

Israel – the former slaves and escapees from Egypt whom God chose as His special people; about Israel's kings, especially King David, Bethlehem-born and Jerusalem-based; about the visions and voices of the ancient Hebrew prophets who dreamed, hoped and envisaged the astonishing things that God would one day do to save His people from their exile in sin and judgment. This is why Matthew offers us such a profoundly intriguing beginning to his story of Jesus.

In as many words, Matthew insists from the start that the coming of Jesus was truly 'an idea whose time had come'. The divine promise had gestated in the womb of Israel's history for 1,900 long years. Divine seeds had been germinating in the soil of the human story until *that* year and *that* Child.

ISRAEL'S VOCATION AND DESTINY

We need to be alert for Matthew's characteristic way of putting this when he speaks of 'prophecy being fulfilled'. Such 'fulfilment terminology' or formulae is typical of Matthew's presentation of the Jesus story.[1] At this point we need to exercise some care. The language of 'fulfilment' does not mean that there are predictions about Jesus in the Old Testament in the form of occasional proof-texts, which then became true of him because they happily land on target. Rather, the word implies that the whole pattern of Israel's story is being gathered up and reproduced in Jesus, filled up to the full by His very birth, ministry, death and resurrection. Uniquely then, Jesus perfectly embodies the vocation and destiny of Israel itself. This is why Matthew begins with his genealogy. It is, in effect, a 'condensed history of Israel'.[2]

Nor does fulfilment mean that Matthew is writing up stories to fit Old Testament predictions, as some critics have alleged. If he was then, frankly, he was rather ham-fisted to say the least. No, it was the events themselves that suggested the earlier scriptures, not the other way round. Matthew's revelatory breakthrough came when he was given to see that *the story of Jesus was the climax of Israel's history, bringing it to its divinely intended goal.*

And so Matthew sets out to show how Jesus re-enacts the whole pattern of events in Israel's history, in order to bring that history to its God-appointed completion and in so doing to fulfil the purpose for which Israel was chosen by God in the first place. He does this in two distinct ways in the opening two chapters of his Gospel account: by way of *Genealogy – People* (Matt. 1), and *Geography – Places* (Matt. 2).

GENEALOGY – PEOPLE

We first look at Matthew 1:1–17. The only way to begin to understand the story of Jesus is to see it as part of the older story about Israel found in the Old Testament record. Matthew presents a simplified version of this history in three epochs or stages:

- *Stage One* runs from Abraham to David – Abraham being the one in whom 'all the nations will be blessed'.

- *Stage Two* is from David to the Exile – David, the king who was to embody the national destiny of Israel.
- *Stage Three* brings the story from the Exile to Jesus – the Babylonian Exile, prophetically understood by the prophets as the 'death' of the nation.

This condition was only partially relieved by the physical return of the exiles to the land in the fifth century BC. Its unresolved issues of sin and forgiveness, its unredeemed hopes of the renewal of God's people as a new covenant community and the return of God as king waited their moment of realisation. The Exile with its profound unmet needs and prophetic dreams – as a continuing state of affairs for Israel – thus formed the immediate springboard for the coming of Jesus.

Our attention is drawn to the presence of women in Jesus' family tree. Rather than naming the matriarchs of Israel – Sarah, Rebekah, Leah and Rachel – Matthew highlights four *foreign* women. He does this, suggests Frederick Dale Bruner, because one of his 'purposes is to attack racial and national chauvinisms in the people of God ... Racial prejudice is condemned on the opening page of the New Testament'.[3] Others suggest that the presence of the foreign women is a clear sign of the inclusion of Gentiles in the saving plan of God, or simply that they are included despite the fact that 'none of them fits in with the way things are "supposed" to be'.[4]

It is interesting to note, in passing, some fascinating nuances that Matthew may have been making here. If the generations mentioned in verse 17 are taken as comprising three times fourteen or six times seven generations, then either way Jesus starts the final and perfect seventh generation. In other words, this verse is strongly suggestive of a new genesis or beginning that has taken place with His coming and that echoes the opening verse, which speaks, literally, of the 'genesis of Jesus Christ'. In Frederick Dale Bruner's words, 'Jesus is *Alpha* as well as Omega, *genesis* as well as Telos. Jesus is not only the end and the goal, he is the beginning and origin of God's purposes with the world.'[5]

Be that as it may, from what we have seen so far, the backdrop of Exile in Babylon is clearly formative for the evangelist's understanding of Jesus. This lends weight to the good news that Jesus 'will save his people from their sins' (Matt. 1:21) by bringing Israel's long 'spiritual exile' to an end and ushering in the Messianic era for the world. In this climactic way, God is encountered in Jesus as Immanuel, God with us (Matt. 1:23). The One Creator God Who has travelled with His people for good or ill, camping and decamping in the wilderness, making His presence felt by cloud and fire over tabernacle and in Temple, Whose glory appeared in Babylon to convince His people He had not finally deserted them, *this* God, Israel's Redeemer, is now with them in a unique and unprecedented way. 'The best of all', said the dying John Wesley, 'is that God is with us.'

It's perhaps worth pointing out that the text from Isaiah quoted by Matthew (Isa. 7:14; Matt. 1:23) is not a Messianic prophecy but, in its original context, is a word to King Ahaz that the imminent defeat of his enemies would be a sure sign of 'Immanuel', of God being with him. Matthew therefore sees in Jesus the ultimate sign of God-being-with-His-people. How much more 'with-His-people' can God become than to actually be one of them in flesh and blood? Matthew will end his Gospel on the same significant note. In the continuing presence of Jesus, the missional Church in its ongoing task of making disciples can enjoy the Immanuel experience (Matt. 28:20).

GEOGRAPHY AND PLACES

This second main section of Matthew's story is an echo chamber of Old Testament allusions. Let's take a look at Matthew 2:1–23. Four geographical references make the necessary theological points:

- verses 1–12: Bethlehem (Micah 5:2);
- verses 13–15: Egypt (Hosea 11:1);
- verses 16–19: Exile – Babylon (Jer. 31:15); and
- verses 19–23: Nazareth (possibly Judg. 13:5).

Matthew first depicts Magi travelling from the East, perhaps reflecting the psalmist's prophetic vision of kings bending their knee to the Messianic king: 'The kings of Tarshish and of distant shores will bring tribute to him; the kings of Sheba and Seba will present him gifts' (Psa. 72:10), demonstrating too that the vivid attractiveness of Israel to the world is now capable of fulfilment. And when it comes to the future it's back to Bethlehem, the birthplace of King David: 'But you, Bethlehem, in the land of Judah, are by no means least among the rulers of Judah; for out of you will come a ruler who will be the shepherd of my people Israel' (Matt. 2:6; Micah 5:2).

The section that follows, Matthew 2:13–21, provides an overview of the twin poles around which the Old Testament story of Israel effectively revolves: Exodus and Exile. These two historic events bracket Israel's Old Testament story: from the Exodus out of Egypt to the Exile into Babylon. In other words, these two motifs encapsulate the beginning and the end of Israel's story as a fully independent nation.

THE EXODUS MOTIF

Matthew alone of the evangelists tells us that Jesus goes down into and comes up out of Egypt (Matt. 2:13–15). This entry and exit took place as a result of Joseph's dream, just as his patriarchal namesake Joseph had a dream that led to the Israelites being in Egypt. Matthew quotes the words of Hosea: '… out of Egypt I called my son' (Hosea 11:1, ESV), which is a reference by the prophet to the early description of Israel as 'God's son' (Exod. 4:22). It perhaps needs emphasising that Matthew does not utilise Hosea's words because he sees them as a prediction being fulfilled. When Hosea spoke them, he was not making a prediction at all but offering a moving historical reflection on Israel's great Exodus from Egyptian captivity. This is the connection Matthew seizes on.

Frederick Dale Bruner states it powerfully:

> The most important fact for Matthew about the life of Jesus in this chapter is that Jesus, even before He could Himself consciously act, was led by divine providence to a retracing of the steps of failed Israel, to take up into Himself the aborted call of His people, to be the final Moses-Deliverer, the authentic Joshua-Saviour, the real Davidic-king – the Man. Jesus is what Israel was meant to be.[6]

How fascinating then that Jesus recapitulates Israel's story by beginning where it began: in Egypt. He comes up 'out of Egypt' as the true Israel Son of God. Already Matthew makes us realise that a new and greater Exodus is under way involving a new and greater 'son'.

THE EXILE MOTIF

Matthew then picks up the other end of the Old Testament story of Israel by referring to the traumatic events of the Exile to Babylon. An aching lament of the prophet Jeremiah fills Matthew's mind at this point: 'A voice is heard in Ramah, weeping and great mourning, Rachel weeping for her children and refusing to be comforted, because they are no more' (Matt. 2:17–18; Jer. 31:15). The prophet pictures Rachel, the original mother of Israel, weeping for her descendants who were forcibly removed to Babylon. Jeremiah 31, significantly enough, features the promise of the *new covenant* and speaks of hope beyond the Exile in a context where Ephraim–Israel is called 'God's son' (see Jer. 31:17, 31).

There is firm evidence in Nehemiah 9, in intertestamental Jewish writings, as well as in the Qumran scrolls (created by a Jewish community in that place, who called themselves 'The New Covenantors') that such Jewish thinkers as these believed Israel to be *spiritually still in Exile.*[7] In which case Matthew's intentions become even more clear in claiming: 'he will save his people from their sins' (Matt. 1:21). He is signalling that the child to be born will bring about the real forgiveness and long-awaited restoration of Israel. He will facilitate its release from the Exile of sin and judgment – of which the earlier, physical return to the homeland was but a token. Momentously, this child will renew and restore Israel as God's new covenant community.

The return from Exile motif is reinforced by Matthew in the opening verses of his third chapter, in which the wildly attired John the Baptist is seen to fulfil the Isaianic role of herald, suddenly announcing the return of God as King. Already the profound significance of what this child will achieve – an even greater exodus from slavery and restoration from exile – is painted in the very details of the infancy narrative. It's clear that Jesus will gather up both ends of the Israel story, beginning where it starts in Egypt and restarts in Exile, returning it not merely to the land but bringing it back and restoring it to the God of Abraham, Isaac and Jacob.

In due course, Jesus' baptism (Matt. 3:13–15) will demonstrate his total and public identification with Israel as He commits Himself to 'fulfil all righteousness' and is 'numbered with the transgressors'. Jesus incarnates the covenant integrity of God and embodies the perfect, obedient, covenant response of God's people.

CHAPTER TWO

Great Expectations – Luke's Story

Read Luke 1–2

We have seen how Matthew tells the world's best story as a very Jewish story. We now turn to Luke to see how he tells a quintessentially Jewish story as the world's story. He aims to show the implications of this Jewish story for the whole Gentile, non-Jewish world: presenting Jesus as 'a light for revelation to the Gentiles and for glory to your people Israel' (Luke 2:32). So he sets his narrative firmly on the world stage:

> In those days Caesar Augustus issued a decree that a census should be taken of the entire Roman world.
>
> Luke 2:1

> In the fifteenth year of the reign of Tiberius Caesar – when Pontius Pilate was governor of Judea, Herod tetrarch of Galilee, his brother Philip tetrarch of Iturea and Traconitis, and Lysanias tetrarch of Abilene ... the word of God came to John ... in the desert.
>
> Luke 3:1–2

In telling his account, Luke writes as a reputable and accountable researcher whose methods have integrity in the public domain. He sets the scene for the events surrounding the coming of Jesus on the broadest canvas. What happens in Bethlehem, Nazareth and Jerusalem will be played out on the world stage. The irony is acute. Little did Augustus Caesar realise that a large stone was being dropped in his political pond and that the ripples would reach Rome. When the emperor decides everyone must be taxed, then every one moves. But one insignificant couple whose names appear on some remote register are moving in response to higher authority even than Caesar (Luke 2:1–3). The arms of Rome stretch to every corner of its far-flung empire and no one is unaffected; but the arm of God is being stretched forth too, and imperial politics unwittingly serve the divine purpose. Whatever decrees later issue from Tiberius Caesar, ensconced amid the comfort zone of his senate, the uncomfortable voice of God will be spoken in the Judean desert by a lonely prophet called John the Baptiser (Luke 3:1). If this had ever been brought to Tiberius' attention, he would no doubt have brushed it aside as a trivial irrelevance. 'But what, Tiberius', asks James Stewart, 'if we have to tell you that the lonely evangelist with the name of John will be a hero and a household word to millions and a shining light of men, long after your own proud name and memory are but the merest blur on history's page?'[1]

So in telling the world's new story, Luke consciously narrows his focus down to an obscure backwater of the empire, to Judah, as well as to a couple of minor characters. As Tom Wright has observed: 'No Roman Emperors, no State occasions, no flourish of Hellenistic trumpets; just a pious, elderly Jewish couple, in the latter days of Herod, longing for a child.'[2]

While John in his Gospel takes the origins of Jesus back to the eternal Word and Wisdom of God, by which the world was created; and while Matthew connects Jesus to the epic Abrahamic beginnings of God's promise, which launches the story of faith, what stance is Luke taking? He proceeds to evoke the birthing of Israel's monarchy, no less. In so doing 'the reader is plunged into the world of Ruth, the Judges, and Samuel'.[3]

In fact, Luke is both reworking and paralleling the narratives of Davidic kingship in the nation of Israel. It's no accident therefore that Zechariah and Elizabeth mirror the accounts of Elkanah and Hannah in 1 Samuel 1:1 and 2:11. This time, however, it's the father, Zechariah, not the mother, Hannah, who is in the house of the Lord. And whereas Hannah presented herself to the priest, Zechariah is himself the priest.

We may summarise these and other intriguing parallels in Luke's narrative thus:

1 SAMUEL 1:1–2:11 **Elkanah and Hannah**	LUKE 1 **Zechariah and Elizabeth**
A couple without children (1:2)	A couple longing for children (1:7)
Hannah in the sanctuary – before a priest (1:9)	Zechariah in Temple – as a priest (1:5,8)
Praying with assurance – that prayers have been heard (1:12,17)	Praying with assurance – of prayers heard (1:13)
Hannah dumbstruck (1:12,13)	Zechariah made dumb (1:20)
Samuel to be a Nazirite (1:11,22)	John to be a Nazirite (1:15)
Samuel is named (1:20)	John is named (1:59–63)
Hannah's song (2:1–10)	Zechariah's song (1:67–79)

In this fascinating 'remake' of the royal story of Israel's kings, it becomes clear that 'John the Baptist is playing "Samuel" to Jesus' "David"'.[4] The outworkings of this involves both judgment and grace. Let's consider these in turn.

A WARNING OF JUDGMENT TO COME

The advent of Samuel spelt judgment both on the house of Saul, the current king in Israel, and also on the corrupt and compromised priesthood of Eli and the ministry of the sanctuary. Likewise, the emergence of John and Jesus heralds a parallel judgment on Herod and the house of Israel, together with the Temple hierarchy in Jerusalem – a judgment later voiced publicly by both John the Baptist and by Jesus Himself.

A PROMISE OF GRACE AND SALVATION TO COME

The advent of Samuel also brought the coming of David, whom the prophet anointed with the sacred oil for the role of king. David was the one on whom the Spirit came with royal endorsement and empowering (1 Sam. 16:3,13). Similarly, John the Baptist would single out Jesus as 'the coming One' by baptism. And Jesus would receive His anointing as King in full measure.

Just as the young David, flushed with the anointing ventured forth to face the gargantuan Goliath in close combat, so Jesus in the full power of the Spirit will be thrust forth to do one-on-one battle with Satan himself in the harsh Judean wilderness. And as David led his bunch of misfits to Jerusalem, Jesus in similar fashion would lead his motley band of disciples there too for the final, defining showdown.

Thus notice is hereby given to Rome and Jerusalem that there is a new kingdom, the kingdom of Israel's God, and that the baby announced by Gabriel, the young man anointed at the Jordan, is to be the King to establish this kingdom.[5] In all this, John the Baptist – like Samuel – had a pivotal role to play since they both mark the return of the prophetic Spirit in their respective eras.

It's worth noting that after 400 years of relative silence, the return of what New Testament scholar Joachim Jeremias once called the 'quenched Spirit' significantly parallels the end of the 400-year period of the judges and the emergence of kingship in Israel. Luke therefore brings to our attention this dramatic fact: the Word of the Lord is being spoken with true prophetic force and penetration once again – with the Baptist (Luke 3:1–3). And this occurs precisely, as with Samuel, at a time when 'the word of the LORD was rare' (1 Sam. 3:1,19ff.). Luke does not allow us to overlook Zechariah and Anna the prophetess, who also add their voices to this new, prophetic chorus (Luke 1:67; 2:36). Nor can we miss the touch of irony whereby dumbness, as much as special words spoken, is a sign of the prophetic voice.[6] It signifies the stopping of human mouths and the opening of God's – and usually means that the prophet has seen a vision (Luke 1:22).

UNUSUAL ACTIVITY

Evidence of the prophetic Spirit's return is found in the unusual activity that accompanies his Presence (Luke 1:15–17). The Holy Spirit clearly has a leading role in the forming of the Christmas story: inspiring, envisioning and guiding. The prophetic Spirit can also be said to inspire the preparation of a prophetic remnant, a people prepared for the Lord (Luke 1:16,17). Such a remnant is already intimated by the waiting group of pious, devout believers such as Elizabeth, Zechariah, Simeon and Anna, all of whom would form the nucleus of the renewed Israel within the still unreconstructed Israel.

By way of summary, Tom Wright helpfully concludes that 'Luke is telling the story of Jesus as the fulfilment, the completion, of the story of David and his kingdom'.[7] Should any be needed, further support for this conclusion comes from a consideration of the royal Davidic motif at the annunciation:

2 SAMUEL 7	LUKE 1
'name great' (7:9)	'great' (1:32)
'throne of his kingdom' (7:13)	'throne of his father David' (1:32)
'be my son' (7:14)	'Son of the Most High' (1:32)
'house … kingdom' (7:16)	'reign over the house of Jacob' (1:33)

We conclude this chapter by drawing out some further parallels – this time between the births of John the Baptist and Jesus in Luke's Gospel:

JOHN	JESUS
Unexpected for parents!	
Zechariah and Elizabeth – barren (1:7)	Joseph and Mary – unmarried (1:27)
Angel Gabriel appears	
to Zechariah (1:11ff.)	to Mary (1:26ff.)
Parents troubled but told not to fear	
(1:12,13)	(1:29,30)
Given a name and promised greatness	
(1:13,15)	(1:31–32)
Both ask 'How?'	
Zechariah (1:18)	Mary (1:34)
Both given signs	
Zechariah (1:20)	Mary (1:36)
Both given songs	
Zechariah's 'Benedictus' (1:67–79)	Mary's 'Magnificat' (1:46–55)
Their children grew strong	
John (1:80)	Jesus (2:40,52)

For Luke then, like Matthew, Jesus is the King Whose time has come. For this is the day of fulfilment and the favourable year of the Lord. This is the day of salvation. 'Today in the town of David a Saviour has been born to you; he is Christ the Lord' (Luke 2:11). The hour has finally arrived for the One Who is the rightful King of the Jews *and* rightful Lord of the nations to be born. He will prove beyond doubt His worthiness to be the long-awaited Servant King. But only at the end of a long, hard road.

For the moment, working men, solid and rough-hewn, tired and ordinary, are alerted to his natal glory and, seizing the moment, come to worship this royal infant. Wise men from the East, long in search of truth, come to the King to submit to His saving wisdom. Waiting greyheads, devout men and women who have prayed for this day to come, give their devotion to the King Who now gives meaning to their lifelong quest, the King Whose time has come. Before the world worships at His feet, these few, the first of many, pay Him homage.

CHAPTER THREE

The Priest Who Lost His Voice

Read Luke 1:5–25

The congregation, gathered for prayer in the Temple courts, was growing restless. What on earth had delayed the priest who was expected to emerge from the sanctuary to pronounce the blessing? Luke's laconic account merely recalls that 'the people were waiting for Zechariah and wondering why he stayed so long in the temple' (Luke 1:21). Suddenly the elderly priest, Zechariah, comes out and looks as if he's just seen a ghost. More than that: he has completely lost his voice. Was this a sudden and bad case of laryngitis or is there some other explanation?

But now what's going on? He's gesticulating strangely and he's trying to tell them something. But he can't – or won't – speak. This is all completely out of character; and the people know it. They begin to sense that something really out of the ordinary must have taken place for the old man to act in this peculiar way. Eventually, the people turn for home without getting their benediction that evening. Later that week, when he had finished his duty roster, the priest too went back home up-country. And he still had not got his voice back. How a man struck dumb might explain these things to his wife we can only guess. Zechariah and Elizabeth had the reputation of being a devoted and, indeed, a devout couple, whose only great sadness in life was that they had no son and heir. In contrast perhaps to some of the hard-bitten professionals running the Temple, they had kept a keen faith alive. They lived faithfully with God as their audience, keeping the commandments with a clear conscience (1:6).

This particular week had been a great one for Zechariah. The Temple was still in the process of being rebuilt following the initiative of Herod the Great. But teams of priests conducted its services – up to 18,000 divided into 24 divisions (see 1 Chron. 24:1–19) – who took it in turns to come to Jerusalem to take prayers for two weeks each year. With such a huge number of priests available, it became a once-in-a-lifetime honour for a priest to be assigned to this duty. What a sense of privilege, then, Zechariah must have felt as he set out: to be chosen by lot to offer the incense on the altar in the holy place (Luke 1:9). And what a story he would have to tell Elizabeth when he got back home. She, being a priest's daughter, would certainly share his sense of pride.

At last the moment had come: with the incense's pungent smoke drifting, swirling and wreathing upwards all around him, Zechariah, 'lost in wonder, love and praise', stood alone in the holy place; and the crowds of worshippers outside in the courtyards prayed on (Luke 1:10). Suddenly and without warning Zechariah realised he wasn't alone: 'Then an angel of the Lord appeared to him, standing at the right side of the altar of incense' (Luke 1:11). Zechariah was terrified, scared out of his wits. Is this response typical when religious people are suddenly confronted with a supernatural happening? Before the priest can regain his composure, the angel is telling him incredible things (Luke 1:13–17). He can scarcely believe what he's hearing; such as the shocking – and surely ludicrous – news that a son will be born to Elizabeth and himself; that this son will be the herald of the coming salvation of the Hebrew people; that his prayers for the saving of Israel are actually about to be answered.

Now while this may be regular good news to an angel, it sounds to a devout man like Zechariah just too good to be true. And so in his startled state he blurts out his disbelief: 'How can I be sure of this? I am an old man and my wife is well on in years' (Luke 1:18). The dialogue that follows is not without its amusing side. Zechariah's first thoughts are about the doubtful condition of his procreative powers; the angel tells of his own privileged place next to the Ever-Living God. The dialogue runs from the impossible to the possible: '"I am an old man" … "I am Gabriel" …' and God is God! The priest's lack of conviction earns him no credit with the angel, who responds by rendering him speechless 'until the day this happens'.

And when at last Zechariah recovers enough to grope his way out to the waiting crowds, he has indeed lost his voice and they have lost their benediction. Zechariah has been privileged to hear 'leaked information' about the most stupendous blessing that would ever come from God. Unbelief is rendered speechless so that 'every excuse may die on the lips of him who makes it and no living man may think himself beyond the judgment of God' (Rom. 3:19, Phillips). But this is the beginning of good news because our speechlessness is the prerequisite for God's word to be heard.

Here is a clear sign for us that the old priesthood and revelation must give way to the Incarnate Word Himself. From now on it will be Jesus Who definitively blesses the people, as Luke records: 'When he had led them out to the vicinity of Bethany, he lifted up his hands and blessed them' (Luke 24:50).

As a consequence of making the full, final and sufficient sacrifice for sin, after being raised up in newness of resurrection life, and immediately before He ascends to the Father, Jesus becomes *the* final priest by bestowing His lasting and life-giving benediction upon His waiting disciples.

As for Zechariah, he could give no blessing to the people; for on them was coming a blessing greater than anything they or he, a trustworthy priest, could pray for. From that blessed night and for the next nine months Zechariah was just *too blessed to give a blessing.* What doesn't leave you speechless will never set you singing.

JOHN THE BAPTIST – MAN OF DESTINY

The vision and the voice that stunned Zechariah into silence unveiled the miracle and destiny of a son to be born to him and Elizabeth. The child is to be named 'John'. To be a father at long last would bring Zechariah immense joy. And what prospective parent wondering how their progeny might turn out would not have warmed to the prospect of their son bringing joy to many.

Beyond being a personal blessing, the angel evaluates the boy's historic significance. First, Zechariah is told that his child is *marked out for greatness* (Luke 1:15). What Luke had in mind was not the greatness that would attract the world's acknowledgment or recognition. It was a greatness that was to be perceived only 'in the sight of the Lord'. For the true measure of greatness is how the Lord evaluates us. Think of that when we next read the outstanding obituary notice of some great public person. Before the world, people like Zechariah and Elizabeth were nobodies, but before the Lord they were 'righteous before God' (ESV). In other words, what we are before God is what really counts.

Our media age puffs up with false fame, hypes up superstars in a phony firmament, parades big fish in small pools, celebrates puny celebrities swollen-headed by minor achievements. As T.S. Eliot once said of another writer, 'extraordinarily good, but the scale is small'. Bubbles of conceit and self-aggrandisement need to be regularly pricked. 'Whoever humbles himself like this child is the greatest in the kingdom of heaven' (Matt. 18:4). The greatness of John owed nothing to his attire (which with his diet was admittedly unusual), his education or achievements but everything to the fearlessness of his radical message. John's unflinching 'political incorrectness', in confronting Herod with his blatant immorality, led eventually to his death. Above all his greatness would be measured by his dedication to the task of pointing to Jesus and promoting His cause.

UNCOMFORTABLE QUESTIONS

No higher endorsement of John would be possible than Jesus' own commendation: 'There is no-one greater than John' (Luke 7:28). For our part, we can be encouraged by the words that follow: '*yet* the one who is least in the kingdom of God is greater than he'. Uncomfortable questions, however, may still need to be faced, such as: Who do we live our lives for? What audience are we playing to? In what direction do our lives point?

Second, there was John's sheer *dedication*. This attribute is indicated by a future total abstinence (Luke 1:15) as well as 'go[ing] on before the Lord, in the spirit and power of Elijah' (Luke 1:17). While the latter may speak for itself, the former was a precondition of anyone taking the Nazarite vow (Num. 6:3–4; Judg. 13:4–7 – re Samson; Luke 7:33). The suggestion has been occasionally made that John had connections with the Essenes – a Jewish ascetic sect that originated in the second century BC and came to an end in the second century AD. This suggestion remains unproven.

What, however, is beyond argument is that John the Baptist represents the uncompromisingly sharp, countercultural edge of the kingdom of God. He has no wish to be part of the social scene of his day. Instead he heads straight for the Judean desert. And in that barren place of wilderness he immediately identifies himself with the austere beginnings of Israel – and sets about making himself the rallying-point for a rededication to the vocation of being God's radically different people.

Later on, Jesus counters people's reaction to John's wild appearance and scary message, asking: 'What did you go out into the desert to see?' The Baptist certainly didn't model a soft lifestyle, or a flabby spirituality, let alone offer a cheap grace. Rather, he invited the people, as Joshua had once done, to come to the Jordan and to consecrate themselves afresh to God in a baptism of repentance for forgiveness of their sins. So the 'renewed Israel' might cross over into the new 'promised land' of God's kingdom.

The key to the effectiveness of John's mission would be his *empowerment by God's Spirit.* He was in fact to be filled with the Spirit while in his mother's womb (Luke 1:15c,41). Such empowerment is the indispensable requirement for any prophet. And the measure of John's empowerment by the Spirit is that of an earlier and equally rugged prophet of Yahweh: Elijah (Luke 1:17).

It was Elijah who came on the scene at a crucial, critical moment in Israel's history. No wonder, then, that Jewish expectation was on tiptoe for someone 'in the spirit and power of Elijah'; for another searing prophet to reappear, Elijah-like, *to mark the End of the Ages.* So it was that John, from the earliest moment possible, became powerfully filled with the prophetic Spirit of the new Messianic Age.

In the fourth place, John was to have a *distinctive mission.* It was primarily to turn many of the people of Israel back to the Lord their God (see Luke 1:16,17). A people who had grown complacent and comfortable –

and had become self-deluded into the bargain – needed to be sharply confronted with the distance that had grown up between them and the God Whom they worshipped. John was called to close the credibility gap between what they were professing and what they were practising. Such a 'turning' ministry as this evokes an exilic scenario, but returning to a physical land 500 years before was one thing; returning the chosen people to the Lord was a much deeper issue that required a resolution here and now, once and for all. John's mission was also 'to turn the hearts of the fathers to their children' (see Luke 1:17b).

EVERY GENERATION

Turning parental hearts towards their children meant, literally, repairing dysfunctional families and homes, rebuilding domestic harmony, restoring relationships. In short: bridging the generation gap. For the coming of the day of salvation heralds the hope of healing for the generations, overcoming the vicious wedge driven between the generations by the notions of freedom and independence foisted on them by a pagan culture; bringing to an end abusive and emotional distancing through parental domination, so that hearts are melted towards children in every generation.

Another 'turning' aspect of John's ministry was 'to turn … the disobedient to the wisdom of the righteous' (Luke 1:17c). This means closing the moral and ethical gap that so discredits the testimony of God's people before a watching world. With holy passion, the Baptist will recall God's people to ways of covenantal living that exhibit the righteousness of God, to wise ways of thinking and behaving that enhance the reputation of their God, to re-establishing habits of heartfelt obedience that demonstrate, unequivocally, that they have broken with their idolatries and joyfully pay allegiance to the Lord their God.

'Turning' or converting people was John's calling. Nearer to our own time, Charles Finney once remarked:

> A revival (of religion) is indispensable to avert the judgment of God from the Church. The fact is that Christians are more to blame for not being revived than sinners are for not being converted.

This observation finds its echo in the motto for the Welsh Revival: '*Bend the Church and save the world*'.

By way of summary, let's now tease out some specific indicators regarding the unique significance of John the Baptist in relation to the Old Testament Scriptures. For example, John becomes a leading figure in a historic and *significant event*. Just as Daniel was praying when the angel Gabriel appeared to him (Dan. 9:20ff.), so John's father, Zechariah, while ministering at the altar of incense, was visited by Gabriel. This great angel's visitations always signalled an event of apocalyptic proportions, indicating that a major turning-point in the story of God's kingdom was about to happen, a moment when the curtain of heaven is turned back and earthly realities are given eternal significance. John's birth becomes just such a moment.

Then there is John's *significant role.* This has clear parallels with the function of Samuel. Both he and John were probably committed at an early age to the Nazirite vow (1 Sam. 1:22 is suggestive of this for Samuel; also the same verse in a Qumran text ends with the words: 'a Nazirite for ever all his days'). As for John, his ascetic lifestyle – 'never to take wine or other fermented drink' (Luke 1:15) – his uncut hair and unkempt appearance have all the classic marks of a Nazirite, one who is completely consecrated to Yahweh, who regards his body as holy. The role of the Baptist is to be preparatory, as Samuel's role was regarding David. John is to mirror the role of his ancient prophetic predecessor, no less. He was to be as 'Samuel' going before the new 'David' – to anoint Jesus as King over Israel.

John's ministry is further characterised by having one, overall, *significant aim.* It was to prepare the people of Israel for the coming of Jesus and His kingdom – He Who was to be more powerful than Elijah-spirited John. Such preparatory ministry is spoken of by Malachi (Mal. 2:6; 3:1; 4:4–6). To this end, John 'exhorted the people and preached the good news to them' (Luke 3:18).

There is no doubting, finally, John the Baptist's *significant impact.* He would be not only instrumental in bringing joy and delight to his parents, but also the cause of much rejoicing by the Jewish people (Luke 1:14). Of course someone like Herod would have good reason to quail in his sandals at some of John's utterances. But because John's desert proclamation preludes the long-awaited Messianic era, we may also reckon for *great joy* to be the mark of its acceptance by those who were among the righteous in Israel (Luke 1:76,77).

CHAPTER FOUR

The Priest Who Found His Voice – as a Prophet

Read Luke 1:57–80

'*Dumb priest speaks*' is how a tabloid subeditor might have headlined this section of Luke's narrative (1:57–79). It begins with the safe birth of a male child to Elizabeth. This is viewed by her relatives and neighbours as a great mercy from the Lord God, giving rise to an outpouring of shared joy (Luke 1:58). Then, eight days later and at the same time as his circumcision, the all-important naming of the child was to take place. Elizabeth surprises everyone by declaring that his name is to be 'John'. So they remind her that no one among her relatives had that particular name.

To settle the matter they turn to the boy's father, who takes hold of the wax-covered board on which he'd been writing messages for the last nine months. To their complete astonishment he scrawls: 'His name is "John"' – the name given by the angel. The instant Zechariah's obedience is in 'print', his dumbness leaves him. *He has found his voice, which unbelief had closed* (Luke 1:20). Immediately the old priest is filled with the Holy Spirit and his mouth overflows with prophetic praise (Luke 1:67).

Nine months late as he is, Zechariah finally pronounces his benediction (Luke 1:67–79). His song is addressed to God in thanksgiving for the fulfilment of the Messianic hopes, and also for the infant John, who is to be the Lord's forerunner. In later years this song was entitled *The Benedictus*, which means 'blessed'. At this point a number of important insights need highlighting in Zechariah's wonderful song.

First, *Zechariah sings of God redeeming Israel* (Luke

1:68). Zechariah blesses God – just as David blessed God for Solomon's accession to the kingdom (1 Kings 1:48). He then declares that God has 'come and has redeemed his people'. The word 'come' translates the Greek word *episkeptomai* (from which we get 'episcopal' and 'bishop': one who watches over). It can therefore speak of God 'watching favourably' on Israel for its redemption.

Of course, in the biblical story the word 'redeemed' is a term with a long and precious history, recalling the Exodus in particular. It resonates with notions such as the setting of slaves free by payment of a price, of being released from prison and given the freedom to love and breathe again.

Second, *Zechariah sings of God raising up a Saviour* (Luke 1:69–71). The phrase 'to raise up' is very reminiscent of the judges, who were raised up to lead Israel in its hour of need. Then we have a seemingly curious phrase: 'a *horn* of salvation'. The picture here is that of a horned ox, a symbol of great strength and seen as a token of God's determination to conquer His people's enemies and to win their freedom (see Psa. 18:2c; 89:17; 132:17; and in Hannah's prayer – 1 Sam. 2:10d). Then the remaining words of Luke 1:69, 'in the house of … David', connect us with the vividly prophetic words of the covenant promises made to David (2 Sam. 7:11b–14).

Third, *Zechariah sings of God remembering his covenant* (Luke 1:72,73). From the beginning of the redemptive story, such specific remembering by Yahweh formed the basis for salvation: 'The Israelites groaned in their slavery and cried out, and their cry for help ... went up to God. God heard their groaning and he remembered his covenant with Abraham, with Isaac and with Jacob. So God looked on the Israelites and was concerned about them' (Exod. 2:23–25; see also Psa.105:7–10,42; 106:44,45).

The covenant spoken of in these passages is the fundamental one that God made with Abraham and that was to become the very backbone of the Bible itself. We will always misunderstand the Old Testament if we fail to see what Paul and other New Testament writers clearly saw: that the Abrahamic covenant is more fundamental to God's purposes than the Mosaic covenant – and the Torah itself discloses this cardinal fact. There are four components to the Abrahamic covenant, which are indicated in the Genesis narrative, in Genesis 12–22:

- *Promises* (Gen. 12) – these are promises of blessing, descendants and land.
- *Covenant* (Gen. 15) – established on the basis of God's word and Abram's belief in it (Gen. 15:6), thus bringing him into covenant relationship with God. This was 'credited to him as righteousness', the latter word being a relational term used throughout the Old Testament and, specifically, implying a covenantal relationship with Yahweh, Who secures it with an elaborate and ancient covenant ritual involving blood sacrifice (Gen. 15:18).
- *Circumcision* (Gen. 17) – this being the outward and visible sign of being in the covenant family. We recall that Zechariah's song is set on the day of

John the Baptist's circumcision (Luke 1:59).

- *Oath* (Gen. 22) – God swears an oath, and in so doing guarantees the commitment, the promises that he has made to Abraham – recalled in Zechariah's song (Luke 1:73).

Once again we see this vivid song celebrating the culmination of long-term planning and long-term covenantal commitments on God's part. Salvation, when it comes, is not a bolt from the blue; it is not a desperate remedy hastily put together when things turn out for the worse. Salvation is the unfolding of the covenant promises first made to Abraham and reiterated to Israel at Sinai, to forge a people who would 'serve him without fear in holiness and righteousness' all their days (Luke 1:74b,75).

Precisely on this rests the hope of the entire Gentile world; this is the reason for Jesus coming into the world.

> For I tell you that Christ has become a servant of the Jews on behalf of God's truth, to confirm the promises made to the patriarchs so that the Gentiles may glorify God for his mercy, as it is written:
>
> 'Therefore I will praise you among the Gentiles; I will sing hymns to your name.'
>
> Again, it says, 'Rejoice, O Gentiles, with his people.'
>
> And again, 'Praise the Lord, all you Gentiles, and sing praises to him, all you peoples.'
>
> And again, Isaiah says, 'The Root of Jesse will spring up, one who will arise to rule over the nations; the Gentiles will hope in him.'
>
> Rom. 15:8–12

Fourth, *Zechariah sings of the destiny of his own son* (Luke 1:76,77). John is to be a prophetic forerunner (cf. Mal. 3:1) who will prepare the way of the Lord (cf. Isa. 40:3; Luke 3:4), to herald the end of Israel's spiritual exile. But how will he accomplish this task? By bringing a knowledge and recognition of the Lord and announcing 'the forgiveness of sins' (cf. Isa. 40:1,2; 43:22–44:8; Jer. 31:31,34).

Fifth, *Zechariah sings of the dawning of the day of salvation* (Luke 1:78,79). John will be the unique herald of the dawning day of salvation and grace: the rising sun will come to us from heaven (cf. Mal. 4:2). The defining characteristic of that new dawn is not in a crude display of crushing might, nor a dazzling 'flash in the pan' but in the slow and steady dawning of an inevitable new day of grace. And the phrase 'tender mercy' is the same word (Greek *splanchna*, 'compassion') used when Jesus healed the leper. It signifies the emotional intensity of God's involvement with His people, moving Him to visit them in salvation.

And so with John's emergence, the 'rising sun' seeps across the morning sky – and this sun is now the greater luminary: the 'high King of heaven, heaven's bright Sun', the Christ-Child Himself. He is the Sun that authentically warms our world. No longer are we in the world of Narnia, where C.S. Lewis said it was 'always winter but never Christmas'. Christmas means that the world is now flooded with the warmth of the sun of God's love and tender mercy.

It was Carnegie Simpson who remarked: 'There was indeed a new love which amid the cold of that first

Christmas came to the world like the heat of a midsummer day, and its warmth has never died out from the hearts of men.'

We might add: the great thaw begins. The creative Spirit is active again to melt hearts. Like those Canadian rivers in winter, frozen at the mouth, we thaw out and begin to sing and praise and prophesy again.

This 'rising sun' sheds its light on those who sit in darkness – and again we are linked to the hopes of Israel – to that time when they would be on the other side of the Exile (Isa. 9:1,2). This 'rising sun' gives life, and causes dead things to stir, move and begin to grow, piercing the gloom of death's long shadow. This 'rising sun' floods the future with guidance and vision – to redirect our feet onto the path of God's peace.

And so it was that the priest who had lost his voice found it as a prophet. What a glorious benediction he gave to the world! Certainly it was well worth waiting for. In his own way, Bernard of Clairvaux was to later echo these sentiments, thus:

Jesus, King most wonderful
Thou Conqueror renowned;
Thou Sweetness most ineffable
In whom all joys are found.
When once thou visitest the heart
Then truth begins to shine
The earthly vanities depart
Then kindles love divine.

INTERLUDE

Christmas and Pentecost Compared

At this juncture we pause to reflect on the intriguing parallels between the events of Christmas and those of Pentecost.

There is a waiting group. Each one – Zechariah, Elizabeth, Simeon and Anna – is prayerful and expectant. So were the Eleven, Mary, Jesus' brothers and some other women, as Acts 1:13,14 describes. Significantly, only Mary was in both groups.

There is a supernatural movement of the Spirit. This occurs with John (Luke 1:15), Mary (Luke 1:35), Elizabeth (Luke 1:41), Zechariah (Luke 1:67), and Simeon (Luke 2:25ff.). Similar marks of the Messianic Age – marks that are attended by the empowering Presence of God's Spirit – are found in Luke's account in Acts 1:8; 2:1ff.

There is revelation that heralds Jesus. The Spirit comes to announce and glorify Jesus, beginning with the unborn as the foetal John leaps to see his day (Luke 1:41,44), and then on to quite specific revelation (see Luke 1:31–33; 2:26,30). Acts 2:36 is similarly specific: 'God has made this Jesus, whom you crucified, both Lord and Christ.'

There is an outburst of prophecy and song. Mary is the first to speak and sing with the Spirit's anointing (Luke 1:42,46ff.); then Zechariah (Luke 1:64,67ff.). And on the Day of Pentecost the wonders of God were declared in everyone's mother-tongue (Acts 2:11).

CHAPTER FIVE

East-Side Story

Read Luke 1:26–45

No sooner has Elizabeth – by now in the sixth month of her unexpected pregnancy – opened the door to welcome her younger cousin from Nazareth, than women's talk starts to flow: 'I rushed here as quickly as I could when I heard you were pregnant – to tell you my own amazing news!'

'I'm so glad to see you but should you have risked the journey into these bandit-ridden hills of ours?'

'But there's so much to share. Some amazing things have been happening to me – I'm going to have a baby too and an angel appeared to me to tell me that …'

'I know … I know already!'

Before they can recover from their breathless exchange, Elizabeth's unborn baby is kicking fiercely, she is filled with the Holy Spirit – and immediately proclaims prophetic blessings on Mary in a loud voice.

What a story Luke tells (Luke 1:39–45). Some women's talk! *'Miracle mums meet'* is perhaps how one of the tabloids would have headlined it. The evangelist is more than happy to give the two women a starring role in his Christmas story. Ben Witherington, who has made a special study of the role of women in the Early Church, notes: 'It is Elizabeth and Mary, not Zechariah and Joseph, who are the first to receive the message of Christ's coming, who are praised and blessed by God's angels, and who are first to sing and prophesy about the Christ-child.'[1]

Given the cultural setting of the day, this is remarkable in itself and surely quite deliberate. At this point it is worth noting the general scholarly consensus that while Matthew tells Joseph's story, Luke is telling Mary's version of events.

Witherington goes on:

> Luke represents these women not only as witnesses to the events surrounding the births of John and Jesus, but also as active participants in God's messianic purposes. Perhaps they are also the first examples of the lowly being exalted as part of God's plan of eschatological reversal that breaks into history with, in, and through the person of Jesus.[2]

ELIZABETH OFFERS TWO BLESSINGS

As we reflect on Elizabeth's twin blessings (Luke 1:42–45), it's helpful to recognise that Luke is using two different words for the word 'blessed'. The first word, in verse 42, is the use of the Greek word *eulogeo* in the active participle – because a blessing is being conferred. (In Hebrew the word is *barak*; in Latin *benedictus*; and in English *blessed.*) The second word, in verse 45, is of the Greek adjective *makaria* because an existing state of blessing is recognised, with joy. (In Hebrew the word is *astre*; in Latin *beatus*; and in English *happy, lucky, fortunate.*)[3]

The first blessing (Luke 1:42): 'Blessed are you among women, and blessed is the child you will bear' may be compared with the blessing on Heber's wife, Jael, for her spectacular killing of the cruel Canaanite army commander, Sisera (Judg. 4:21; 5:24–27).

Further comparison can be made with the blessing on Judith, for killing Holofernes, an Assyrian general oppressing Israel: 'O daughter, you are blessed by the Most High God above all women on earth and blessed be the Lord God who made heaven and earth who has guided you to cut off the head of the leader of our enemies' (Judith 13:18).

While such blood-stained incidents as these attracted blessing, Elizabeth's use of the words is for infinitely more peaceful ends altogether. It was typical of Jesus, at some moment in His itinerant ministry, to refocus such a greeting:

> A women in the crowd called out, 'Blessed is the mother who gave you birth and nursed you.' He replied, 'Blessed *rather* are those who hear the word of God and obey it.'
>
> Luke 11:27,28

Of course, Mary did both of these things.

Elizabeth makes a tender response to this unexpected situation: 'Why am I so favoured, that the mother of my Lord should come to me?' (Luke 1:43). As Elaine Storkey has observed, here is a 'recognition that Mary's pregnancy completely overshadows her own; it fulfils her own ... and already this child and his mother are caught up in the reality of all that lies ahead'[4] when Mary's child will have a superior place in Israel's history.

The second blessing (Luke 1:45) – 'Blessed is she who has believed that what the Lord has said to her will be accomplished' – well illustrates Elizabeth's altruism, which Storkey once more notes: 'The generous Elizabeth does not focus on the promises made to her, or on the willingness to believe them. She is far more ecstatic that Mary has believed.'[5]

A GIRL CALLED MARIA

The reason for Elizabeth's profound and perceptive reaction is found in the account of the annunciation (Luke 1:26–38) and the spotlight shines on Mary. Mary – Maria – is probably fourteen years old, living in the Galilean town of Nazareth and betrothed to Joseph, a local carpenter. The condition of betrothal was a middle stage between what we might call engagement and the marriage itself, the time when a couple would be committed to each other but still living apart with their respective families.

Because Jesus would be Joseph's legal son, he was qualified to belong to the 'house of David'. Designated a virgin, Mary had not yet had any sexual relations. Then the angel Gabriel appears on the earthly scene from the very 'Presence of God' (Luke 1:19) to announce the advent of Jesus, as he had previously of John (Luke 1:13–17). As we have noted previously, the angel's appearance has enormous eschatological significance (cf. Dan. 8:16ff.; 9:21ff.).

His first word to Maria is a courteous one: 'Greetings' or 'Hail' (from which greeting is derived: 'Hail, Mary'; in Latin, *Ave Maria*). However, the Greek word for 'Greetings' is *Xaire* and, importantly, implies the notion 'to rejoice'. She is also addressed as 'favoured one' (Greek *kexaritomene*, or 'one who has "found favour or grace with God"', Luke 1:30). Significantly, 'Mary is described as receiving grace, not as endowed with the power to give grace.'[6]

The words 'The Lord is with you' are not only suggestive of the measure of God's favour and honour granted to Mary for undertaking such a task, but also of the quiet assertion that God's own Presence will guarantee it. Perhaps we can also detect a hint of what was disclosed to Joseph that they will have a son 'and they will call him Immanuel – which means, "God with us"' (Matt. 1:23). And what exactly does God guarantee to this young mother-to-be? She will 'give birth to a son'; he will be 'great'; he will be called, 'the Son of the Most High'; he will be given 'the throne of his father David'; and he will 'reign … for ever' (Luke 1:31–35).

In Luke's annunciation narrative, we should be aware of the Davidic overtones of sonship present in the text. What might these overtones be? We must go back to 2 Samuel 7:11–14 where we discover that, as part of the covenant that Yahweh made with David (Psa. 89:3,4), David was promised a house or a dynasty; a throne; an everlasting kingdom; plus a unique father/son relationship.

As far as the king of Israel is concerned he represents collective 'Israel' – God's own first-born son (Exod. 4:22). David was adopted as such at his coronation (Psa. 2:7), and was able to call on Yahweh as 'my Father' (Psa. 89:26,27). Such sonship was then assumed into the greater Sonship of Jesus by the Spirit of holiness at His conception and was confirmed by that same Spirit of holiness at His resurrection from the dead – when He was declared to be the 'Son-of-God-with-power' Son of God. Thus through 'the spirit of holiness', Jesus 'was declared to be Son of God with power' (Rom. 1:3,4, NRSV; cf Luke 1:35).

But this is to get ahead of ourselves in the story. For the moment it is useful to pause and to compare and contrast these prospects for the Lord Jesus with those for John the Baptist in Luke 1:

JOHN	JESUS
Will be great (v.15)	Will be great … Son of the Most High (v.32)
Will prepare people (v.17)	Will rule over people (v.33)
Will be provisional (v.17)	Will be permanent (v.33)
Will be a prophet (v.17)	Will be Son of God (v.35)
Will be filled with the Spirit (v.15)	Will be conceived by the Holy Spirit (v.35)

Suffice it to say that Jesus eclipses John:

- John is the one who prepares the way; Jesus is the Way.
- John is the best man; Jesus is the Bridegroom.
- John is the lamp; Jesus is the Light.
- John is a voice; Jesus is the Word.

CHAPTER SIX

The Child and Madonna

Read Luke 1:26–38

Mary can hardly believe her ears.

Not only is she to have a son but Mary's boy-child is pinpointed as the One in Whom are to be fulfilled the hopes and dreams for the coming of the Messianic King Who is to bring God's kingdom of justice and salvation.

Mary's response is understandable to say the least: 'How will this be since I am a virgin?' (Luke 1:34). No censure is attached to her query as it was Zechariah's unbelief (Luke 1:18). Mary's puzzlement is natural and refreshingly honest. Modern sophisticated skeptics might have responded differently: 'How can anyone in this rational, scientific age believe in this? God, angels, virgin conception – all this is incredible and unbelievable.' And they would of course be absolutely right. But Mary is no fool. She knows where babies came from as well as the next woman, and doesn't need modern critics to tell her she's naive and prescientific. In any case, if people are not going to believe this Christmas stuff, let's make sure they have good reasons for not believing it.

Mary's response encourages us not to sell people short and reduce this scandalous message to something easily acceptable. Like her we want to ask: 'How is this possible?' We remain true to her legacy when we refuse to make it easier to believe by scaling down the miracle of the incarnation to some bland and 'intellectually correct' cliché about harmony and good will. Mary's question is not an unbelieving one, nor will it allow us to settle for anything less than a full-blown mystery. Like a virgin told to expect motherhood, we too come to ask 'how' God's will can be made possible in our life. Or, like a pregnant woman who relishes the prospect of parenthood but wonders why the pain is necessary, we too may ask: 'Why the pain?' In fact, as the answer to both questions, a 'son is better than an explanation'.[1]

Gabriel's answer to Mary's bafflement heightens the mystery by pointing to the supernatural Spirit of God as providing the only explanation for what is about to happen. He highlights three dimensions of the Spirit's activity that follows (Luke 1:35).

THE SPIRIT OF THE KING

The Holy Spirit is *the creative Spirit*. Not, in other words, simply enabling yet another prophetic ministry to function, like others in the past. But here is the concentrated, elemental and creative Spirit of God at work – the 'power of the Most High', no less – initiating a new creation.

The Holy Spirit is *the consecrating Spirit*. The phrase 'will be called holy' or 'the holy one to be born' is not intended to imply that sex *per se* is unclean; or that the virgin birth was the means of avoiding an originally transmitted disease called sin. There is therefore no good reason to suppose that Mary needs the appellation 'immaculate'. The Spirit's function here is to set apart for a special task, empowering for ethical victories by the indwelling of the Spirit. This child will be uniquely holy in His essential relationship with God.

The Holy Spirit is also *the covenantal Spirit.* In the Spirit's 'overshadowing' there are echoes of Exodus 40:35, where 'the divine Spirit is likened to the cloud of God's Presence bringing God's Glory into Israel's camp and leading her through the wilderness towards the Promised Land'.[2] The transfiguration 'cloud' of Luke 9:34 therefore implies nothing less than the new Exodus theme, which is *the covenantal restoration of Israel.*

At this point in the annunciation narrative, Mary's response (1:38) to all the staggering angelic revelations she has just received epitomises the true response of a faithful Israel in delivering Messiah to the world. Through Mary, the Davidic covenant finds its climax and is fulfilled (Luke 1:32ff.); and through Mary, Israel is being remembered by the Lord and is receiving His mercy (Luke 1:54); through Mary the Abrahamic promises are being honoured (Luke 1:55).

And so it is that Mary becomes the true servant of the Lord (Luke 1:38,48).

> To Luke, Mary is this daughter of Zion of the Endtime, the people of God, purified by God's love, where God can be completely at home. In Mary, God can come and live with his people. She is the figure of the Church of the Endtime in which all of us will be found.[3]

Joel Green expresses a similar thought:

> Mary, who seemed to measure low on any social scale –

age, family, heritage, gender, and so on – turns out to be the one favoured by God and the one who finds her identity ultimately in her obedience to God and participation in his redemptive purpose.[4]

MARY'S TWO-FOLD RESPONSE

Mary's response to God's will for her is beautifully enshrined for every succeeding generation in both her speech and her song. Taking *what she said* first, we discover an affirmation of radical servanthood. Mary affirms her willingness to venture boldly on this audacious destiny in wholehearted obedience to the word of the Lord (Luke 1:38ff.). Imitation is said to be the sincerest form of flattery. Mary's embrace of the servant's role is undeniably worth imitating. The essential elements of such servanthood, which she portrays, consist in being:

Open to a defining 'visitation of God' through His special messenger (Luke 1:28). This messenger comes fresh from the very Presence of God. His arrival portends Messianic repercussions. We might well wonder: Was it the dream of every Hebrew girl to be the mother of the Messiah? Maybe so. Yet however much openness to God this desire may imply, it would be another matter altogether to remain open to such an invitation when it actually came, to be willing enough to say 'yes' to such an astounding enterprise. Which begs the question for ourselves: Are we as open as we might be to God's voice?

Overawed by the grace of God (Luke 1:29). It is hard

to believe that Mary would have welcomed the veneration that some branches of the Church universal practise towards her. She is genuinely humbled and amazed by grace – genuinely overawed by the favour that God has so richly bestowed on her (Luke 1:28). As we consider Mary in our own day, we may well ask: Are we touched by the awesome favour of the Most High God that rested upon her? She must surely earn our respect for this alone.

Overshadowed by the Holy Spirit (Luke 1:35). The cloud of transfiguration descends upon the holy mystery of the virgin conception; God's glory at once revealed and concealed. Here is the mystery of life shrouded in the mystery of love; and no more so than in the simplicity of this young, virginal, peasant girl. It is, of course, a great yet also relative wonder that the Holy Spirit creates the life of Christ in us so that we too partake of the mystery of this divine life and love.

The virgin birth stands boldly here, unexplained and impossible to analyse, proclaiming that Christ's true humanity and our new humanness in Him are both without an explanation – apart from God. 'Overshadowed' Mary might have been, but overpowered she was not (contrary to those feminist writers who see unsavoury overtones of rape here). Mary's willing co-operation – her 'yes'– was asked for.

Obedient to the Word of God (Luke 1:38). Suddenly faced with the stupendous responsibilities implicit in Gabriel's message, it was natural for Mary to ask questions, to be hesitant, to have her doubts and 'fears within'. But for her it was enough to be assured that with God no word from Him was impossible of fulfilment (Luke 1:37). This response of faith rightly makes her an enduring, model believer and disciple. The risks she took were enormous: she risked Joseph's rejection, the loss of her reputation in the town, the ostracism of her family and friends, social and religious disgrace.

Such obedient servanthood runs diametrically counter to the culture of our own day. Mary abandons her pride, gives up her small ambitions, dies to the demands of self-interest. It is for these things that we call her 'blessed'. As Elaine Storkey comments: 'Servanthood is not something we choose in opposition to rich independence; it is something we choose in opposition to self-centred arrogance and toil.'[5]

A 'sword', Mary was told, would pierce her soul as a result of her special servanthood. She had yet to face her son's puzzling ambiguity towards her (John 2:4); she had yet to watch Him misunderstood, betrayed and tortured; she had yet to stand beneath His cross of shame as He died His agonising death.

All the time she kept the Word, treasuring it in her heart (Luke 2:19,51), guarding God's investment in her, never denying or disowning it as too inconvenient, too painful or too embarrassing. Then came that glorious day in the upper room when the Holy Spirit came powerfully on all the waiting disciples, including her. As the Spirit had overshadowed her, alone, those many years before, so now Mary experienced that special joy again that she had experienced at the miraculous conception of Jesus. But this time things are different; this time the joy she once felt at His being part of *her* body is eclipsed by the joy of her being part of *His* Body Who is the regnant Messiah of Israel and the Lord of the world.

SINGING MAGNIFICENTLY ABOUT GOD

Mary's response to God is enshrined not only in what she said but in *what she sang* (Luke 1:47–55). Her song celebrates revolutionary salvation. Throughout the song are tightly woven Old Testament threads and echoes of Old Testament songs, especially Hannah's (1 Sam. 2:1–10). The God-directedness of Mary's entire song is impressive. As R.T. France has observed: 'It is a song not about Mary but about God.'[6] And so she declares: '*God* … has done great things for me' (Luke 1:47–49). Mary's soul magnifies God and her spirit rejoices; she is totally and emotionally involved in this heartfelt burst of praise. The greatness of God's salvation and grace is extolled and her own personal reversal of status is relished.

Yet this great reversal is not confined to an individual, however blessed. Such reversal is also national in scale (Luke 1:51–55). There is to be *a political revolution* ('performed mighty deeds with his arm … scattered those who are proud in their inmost thoughts'); there is to be *a social revolution* ('brought down the powerful from their thrones and lifted up the lowly'); there is to be *an economic revolution* ('filled the hungry with good things but has sent the rich away empty').

This revolutionary salvation is God's 'remembering' of Israel as an action of mercy on His part, which is the fulfilment of His age-old promises to Abraham. The pious were not just looking to get something out of it for themselves but for God to come and save His people and bring justice and peace to all. In other words, what fired these faithful people were not personal agendas of self-fulfilment but the ancient covenantal hopes and dreams of the people of God.

Mary is remembered and blessed for her brave obedience in embracing God's will for her life; for willingly playing her part – and paying the price – of bringing Jesus into the world. The very least we can do, in our own way, is gladly to imitate her in that.

ATTITUDES TO MARY

This may be an appropriate point at which to summarise some of the various views and opinions that have arisen around 'this highly favoured lady', Mary.

She is idolised. There are those in the Christian world who seem to come close to idolising if not worshipping her. She is seen as the Queen of Heaven, and as such is the one who can dispense grace. Yet Luke makes it perfectly clear that she is special precisely because she *received* grace.

Nothing separates Protestant believers more from Catholic – even Orthodox – believers than this persistent, iconic emphasis on the Virgin Mary. David Wright, while being a sympathetic observer, nevertheless states: 'More than any other Catholic theological speciality, Mariology labours under a crushing weight of religious crudity, vulgarism, and sheer crass superstition.'[7]

The doctrine of the virgin birth is often utilised to compare Mary with Eve, whereby as death came through the one, so life comes through the other. This sails too dangerously close to the wind of heresy for Protestant ears. It's but a short step from this to making Mary 'co-redemptrix' with Christ in the work of salvation.

She is impersonated. Some sociologists have suggested that it was the repudiation of the cult of Mary in non-Catholic countries that gave rise to the fantasised, ideal and glamorous woman figure that characterises the Hollywood-influenced Western world. The argument proposes that, as in the Middle Ages the Virgin Mary symbolised the values of that age, so now in our consumer-orientated and sexually attuned times, an inverted Mariology takes place, whereby the beauty queen and the page-three girl characterise the values of this age.

In pre-Reformation Europe, it was the Blessed Virgin who dispensed her favours through the system of indulgences. Today the supermodel bestows her unblemished, because retouched, blessing on consumer products – from cars to aftershave – through the professional skills of the advertising industry. If Our Lady at Lourdes can't work you a miracle, the girl in the photo-shoot will, guaranteeing commercial success, sexual prowess, domestic comfort and glamorous holidays. Truly, My Lady has been reinvented as Madonna.

She is ignored. Protestant Christianity has, in the main, turned its back on the Virgin Mary. Radical, secular feminism has currently concurred in this stance since it is held that Mary is overly submissive and too embedded in a patriarchal culture to be taken seriously. Even Catholic feminist theologians despair of making Mary fit theologically, because she is too closely identified with their Church's tragic linkage of sex and original sin (though in a pro-choice debate, some of their number have used her response to the angel Gabriel to present her as a 'patroness of reproductive choice').

Lastly, *she is imitated.* Mary is, of course uniquely 'blessed' (Luke 1:42). Nevertheless, she has to meet the criteria of discipleship just the same (see Luke 11:27,28). So Mary is presented as the model for a true believer (Luke 1:38,45; cf. 2:27,51). She would pay her own price for believing in her Son (Luke 2:35). This would include misunderstanding and ambiguity (Luke 2:41–52, cf. Mark 3:19–21; John 2:3–5). Finally she is gathered into His family at the time of His execution (John 19:25–27). This also indicates that in Jesus' mind, His being part of her body was of lesser importance than her being part of His Body. Acts 1:14 tells us that following her Son's dreadful death, Mary remained faithful and steadfast. Commenting on Luke 1:45, R.T. France quotes the Jesuit scholar J.A. Fitzmeyer, who believes that Mary should be revered as 'the first representative of faith in Luke's account.

The verse expresses a fundamental attitude of all Christians, toward the believing Mother of our Lord.'[8] Would Protestants wish to disagree with this sentiment?

THE UPSIDE-DOWN KINGDOM

Mary highlights for us what can be construed as one of Luke's special emphases: *the reversal of social status*. Rulers are put down, the humble are raised up (Luke 1:52,53). Such reversal is exemplified by Mary herself, for her story is set in an honour–shame culture. In a culture centred on the relative sophistication of Jerusalem, she comes from rural Galilee. In a culture where age is revered, she is unnervingly young (still in her teens). As Joel Green points out,

> She is not introduced as in any way deserving honour. Indeed, her insignificance seems to be Luke's primary point in his introduction of her here, for this is immediately contrasted with Gabriel's declaration of Mary's favoured status (Luke 1:28,30). Within the world of Luke's Gospel, she holds a lofty place in God's eyes. Moreover, she claims a place in God's household (v38). This is her family. That is, she derives her status from God, so that Luke begins here his presentation of a community of God's people whose fundamental social experience is grounded in their relationship to God.[9]

To modern ears, Mary's response is strikingly countercultural. In today's narcissistic climate, 'How can this be …?' would surely have become 'What's in it for me?' 'How relevant is this and how will it affect my life?' And Mary, pondering the magnitude of the treasure entrusted to her, would tell us plainly and eagerly: 'This won't merely affect your life: it will totally change your life!' Jesus is a gift not just for Christmas but for life. Receiving Him is not something that will make life marginally more successful or interesting. You can't add *this* to a list of consumer items and fit into an existing lifestyle.

'Well, it's a private matter; if that's what you believe, that's fine by me but everyone has their own spirituality …' And again Mary will have none of it. This is no private concern, something done in a corner. She sings of the long history of her people, stretching back to Abraham, now reaching its God-ordained goal and climax. She sings of national destinies, of kings and rulers being overthrown and of major upheaval on the world's stage. She celebrates the revolutionary upside-down kingdom of God to be ushered in by her Son, which will put everything right-side up. All this is not some surge of adrenaline in an overwrought young woman overcome with the prospect of being a mother. This is a Spirit-inspired prophetic vision of the turning-point in world history.

And Mary's involvement does not scale down the event to fit into her domestic world. Quite the reverse. This event elevates her domestic world and magnifies her individual significance beyond anything she could have dreamt of. It will do the same for anyone who believes and like her says 'yes' to God's saving plans in Jesus Christ.

So a simple peasant girl from Nazareth is launched into a world-famous figure, caught up in the divine drama of a God Who so loved the world that He gave His only Son for its salvation. Mary is open but not gullible; overawed but not intimidated; obedient but not passive; not a doormat but a willing doorway for 'the Lord Christ to enter in'.

Not for nothing is she deemed 'blessed' among women.

Blessed is everyone who, like her, says an unqualified 'yes' to God, accepts God's Word, opens a life to God's Spirit, and sings the song.

CHAPTER SEVEN

Minding God's Own Business

Read Matthew 1:18–25

It was business as usual. A small businessman in an even smaller town. A worker in wood by all accounts. A menial trade but not a servile one, where a good day's pay could be earned by a hard day's work, much of it routine. He produced simple but robust furniture – tables, chairs, bed frames, stools – and always with the greatest of care. Sometimes he travelled with his trade, doing subcontract work making doors and roof beams for the up-market houses in the affluent and more populous towns of Sepphoris and Capernaum, both less than five miles away. On those occasions he slept on site beneath the stars – and thought wistfully of his own bed.

But at least he could return stocked up with much needed supplies and replacement tools. Local farmers were his regular customers and agricultural implements his speciality: ploughs, threshing sledges, yokes – especially yokes. The family firm of 'Jacob and Sons' had a justified reputation for the smoothest, best-fitting yokes in the area. 'My yokes are easier' had been his father's proud boast; and for once the advertising slogan rang true.

The ancient craft of rural carpentry had changed little since the days, long ago, when the great prophet Isaiah had savagely satirised the idol-makers, carving out their gods from local logs: 'Half the log to fuel the fire to cook the dinner; half the log to fashion the form to make the deity.' How futile this seemed to the carpenter. His people's traditions had taught him that only a living, human being, like a son, could be the chip off the divine block. Being a sincere worshipper of the One True God, he knew that *Israel was God's son*.

Little had changed since Isaiah's time. The tools were the same: the adze, drill, saw, plane, mallet, measuring line and chalk. He never tired of the subtle joys of a silk-smooth edge, a well-joined corner – to say nothing of the varied textures, tints and smells of oak and laurel, cedar and cypress. Once – a year or two back – he had narrowly missed having to make a cross for the Romans. Galilee had been rife with anti-Roman feeling. Rumours of revolution were fermenting, created by bold talk from a few political hotheads no doubt. But one of them had gone too far and the imperial commander was out for summary justice. All this he had learnt later from his fruit-seller friend two doors away. He'd been away when the Roman patrol came hammering at his door. His workmates in Sepphoris had done the job eventually; under duress, or so they said. They'd knocked up a couple of lengths of timber for a cross, using rough-hewn wood to increase the discomfort of the condemned man. Not like my yokes, he thought – though his damaged, work-worn hands reminded him that not even easy yokes come without cost.

Life was not easy, but he was a steady man. Nothing much disturbed him. Except, that is, when his thoughts strayed to the girl he was betrothed to. He dreamed the dreams of an honest man: of love, of a home, of perhaps a son to be apprenticed to the trade who would carry on the family name. Yes, he was settled here. He loved the girl. He was a contented man. *And his familiar world was about to be shattered forever*. The place was Nazareth, the girl was Mary, and the carpenter was Joseph.

It had started like any other day. Axe in hand, he had set out with his donkey for a nearby copse in search of the raw materials he needed. One wonders if he'd had any premonition ('Joseph-bar-Jacob, if you go down to the woods today you're sure of a big surprise'). Was it Mary who told him – perhaps intercepting him on his way back from tree-felling, rushing out in front of the laden donkey on the dusty lane? 'She's pregnant! How can she be? I don't believe it! Who is he? I must know. She says it's God – how can it possibly be God? It's too incredible ... Does she think I'm stupid or something? The angel Gabriel told her! And I'm expected to believe that! And conceived by the Holy Spirit? Poor girl – she must be really out of her mind!'

Even the familiar sights and smells of the workshop did little to calm Joseph's racing brain. His white-knuckled grip on the workbench steadied his body – but not his nerves. Through the unshuttered window, the shafting afternoon sun lit up the fine, swirling sawdust stirred by the violence of his entry. It matched his mood as he slammed the door: turbulent, cloudy, confused.

FACING UP TO A MIRACLE

What should he do? If it was another man then it had to be divorce. No doubt about it. But not the full legal way, in public – he couldn't see her go through that. Perhaps a more private way through a bill of divorcement might soften the blow and lessen the scandal. But knowing her as he did, how could he bring himself to believe the worst of her? Yet if it was hard to believe the worst, wasn't it even harder to believe the best? 'Conceived by the Holy Spirit?! How on earth can I believe that? But, then, what if it's all true …? O God in Heaven, God of Abraham, Isaac and Jacob, help me!'

Let's stand back from this story for a moment. New Testament scholars are agreed that in Matthew's account (Matt. 1:18–25) the focus is fully on Joseph; while in Luke's narrative Mary is the recipient of revelation. In Matthew, then, Jesus apart, Joseph is the key character who receives revelation and through whom the action is moved on. There is no doubting that Joseph's dilemma is acute (Matt. 1:19). But what exactly was it that made him afraid of taking Mary home as his wife? If his suspicions of Mary's adultery were confirmed, then being a just man he would have feared to disobey the law by not divorcing her. If he believed her innocent but knew nothing of the miraculous conception, he could have suspended judgment and learned to live with his great anxiety and uncertainty (in which case it would have been easier if she'd not told him). On the other hand, if he drew back from becoming her husband out of reverent fear for the Holy Spirit's activity, his desire for a family would have to be postponed for some long time.

Of course, none of these attempts to listen in on Joseph's inner debate entirely explain the angel's definite 'Do not be afraid'. After all, who wouldn't be in a confused state of mind, trying to weigh up such unexpected and sobering pros and cons? What really impresses now is Joseph's reaction. He seems remarkably unfazed. Waking up from the dream, Joseph proved himself to be a godly man, for on this issue he was willing, first of all, to listen to God's point of view.

No divine work, no miracle, can truly be understood from the outside. The only way to comprehend a miracle on this scale is from the inside. Which is why God invites us to participate in the biblical drama rather than be mere spectators of it – to come inside and join the cast of His great Story, to read that bit of the script which concerns us, but also to sense the sweep of the plot and the scale of the story line. This is precisely what God did for Joseph. And He did it through the medium of dreams. Dreams were evidently God's way with this man (Matt. 1:20; 2:13,19,22). Biblical dreams have been described as 'God's night messengers', the 'dark speech of the spirit', as effective as the divine method of communication with Joseph here, as with his illustrious patriarchal namesake.

So it is that Joseph – slumped against the wall, emotionally exhausted, unaware of the failing light – falls asleep, his daydreams long since shattered. It's all pure nightmare now. But not for long. As vivid as a voice, the angel commandeers his subconscious to bring him news from the One Whose dreams are bigger and better than our own.

REASSURANCE AND DIRECTION

Immediately there is welcome reassurance and direction: 'Joseph son of David, do not be afraid to take Mary home as your wife, because what is conceived in her is from the Holy Spirit' (Matt. 1:20). Here, confirmed at first hand, is exactly what she had told him but which he'd scarcely dared believe. And it's the message that's most important: 'She will give birth to a son, and you are to give him the name Jesus, because he will save his people from their sins.' Give *us* a night vision, an angel and some startling, personal, divine revelation and the outcome would be only too predictable: an impressive testimony to our own spirituality, followed by a film of the book. Joseph, however, seems commendably underwhelmed by angels and dreams. These notwithstanding, the means of communication are less significant than the events that occasion them; the messengers, however angelic, are of trifling importance beside the magnitude of the message they bring. The miracle of virginal conception is at once more marvellous – and yet more mundane. For what are angels, dreams and private revelations other then sideshows to the main miracle of incarnation?

From this perspective, to follow after angels and signs is to play 'trivial pursuits'. There are those in our own day who dream of angels beating a path to their door, bearing good tidings of health, wealth and prosperity. To them, the angelic message brought to Joseph would seem rather thin gruel. But Joseph is open to better things. For while God is not above blessing our business, He is more eager to bless us with His business. The truth is: *Incarnation upstages us all.* From our vantage point, this side of resurrection, we have even less excuse for overrating angels, dreams and the like. The empty tomb trumps all.

JOSEPH'S REACTION

Joseph's reaction is both impressive and instructive for a second reason: he is willing to be set aside. He is required to embrace a mystery in which he is asked to play a minor role. This means that a family future, in which as husband and father he could look forward to playing the central character, is to be snatched from him. Now a different role is demanded of him: a humbler, more perplexing, more minor yet paradoxically a more responsible one. Forever denied the starring role, Joseph deserves an Oscar for Best Supporting Actor! Was it Bernstein who said that the hardest instrument to play in an orchestra was second fiddle? This is God's gospel from beginning to end, and Joseph's secondary role fits with the miraculous virginal conception.

Also impressive is Joseph's reaction: he is willing to put his reason 'on hold'. He allows his faith take the lead in his search for understanding. This is not because Joseph lived in a prescientific age or was unusually naive and therefore more liable to swallow such fanciful notions as virginal conception than we moderns might. He knew as well as we do that babies are made but one way. That Mary's pregnancy owed nothing to him or to any man was no less credible to him than it would be today. Faith, whether ancient or modern, has to learn the true facts of life. And these are that God is God and nothing is impossible to Him.

Joseph is also willing to swallow his pride. God is telling him (and thereafter the entire world) that while His Son's humanity is needed to bring salvation to mankind, Joseph's manhood is not. In his emphasis on the virgin conception we surely have Matthew's theology of grace teasing us. Joseph was not the last to confront the blunt but saving truth that salvation is not the best we can do for God but the best God can do for us. Indeed, this is the first fact of life in the Christian family: that it is 'by grace we are saved and that not of ourselves: it is the gift of God'. How deeply true for all those children 'born not of natural descent, nor of human decision, or of a husband's will but born of God'.

> Jesus was a son Joseph did nothing to get. Zechariah's getting of John the Baptist was what he could not do without God's special aid; Joseph's getting of Jesus was something he could not do at all, it was wholly the work of God. God, who can of the very stones raise up children to Abraham, and who, when Jesus was dead in the sepulchre, raised him to immortal life … this God first brought Jesus forth from the virginity of Mary, display-

> ing the unmerited and sovereign freedom of his grace; who made the world where no world was, who wonderfully ordained the excellence of man's estate, and yet more wonderfully has restored it.[1]

Salvation, like the newborn child, is not the climax of an evolutionary process but the condescension of God. As P.T. Forsyth put it, salvation 'is not a triumph of our resource but a gift to our poverty'. In being set aside for Mary's virginal conception, Joseph is a fitting symbol of this grace. He is willing to find his significance in the child. The child's life determines his. The child's future settles his. The child's story incorporates his and makes sense of it. In our own age, when self-worth is deemed to be such a priceless commodity, we may be in for some Joseph-like surprises. Those marginalised in whatever sense – the single parent, the homeless, the bereaved, the unemployed, those passed over for promotion – may, just because of their condition, be more open to the meaning and the message of this child. Even God, in Bonhoeffer's words, 'is a God who allows himself to be edged out of this world onto a cross'.[2] Joseph finds life by losing it in this child. Like Joseph, we are more than carpenters through Him Who loves us.

Only a bit part, then, for Joseph – in fact, little more than a walk-on role. But the steps he takes are vital and the lines he speaks sensational. He must, says the angel, do two things: he must give the child a home and a name. First, in giving the child a home and accepting him as his own, Joseph, son of David, becomes the legal father of the child. And in so joining Joseph's family, Jesus is officially linked to the royal dynasty of King David and is legally established in His claim to the throne.

COMPLEMENTED EACH OTHER

In providing a home for Jesus, Joseph was taking on more than he knew: he was to share, with Mary, in the nurture and growth in character of this special child. Austin Farrer has made the point well:

> Christians sometimes talk about Jesus as though he had walked down from heaven a ready-made man, with a complete outfit of true ideas in his head: as though he had only pretended to be a babe in the cradle. But he made a more thorough job of being than that; he needed a mother to smile at him, a father to talk to him, if he were ever going to be a man. Without Joseph and Mary he wouldn't have been anyone on earth.[3]

Which is to say that they complemented each other in the grafting of the divine life onto the stock of our humanity, by divine grace. Through Joseph, Jesus is designated Son of David; through Mary he is begotten Son of God.

But Joseph, second, must give the child a name. A whole theology of salvation underlies Matthew's description of what Joseph was told to do – accepting the presence of Christ as Lord in one's life and naming His Name as the Saviour. And months later it was

Joseph's unique privilege to bend over the infant, incarnate Son of God as the first to utter the name so many millions hold dear: 'Jesus' . *Jesus* is a form of the Hebrew name *Yeshua*, meaning 'God saves', from which the name of Israel's leader into the promised land, *Joshua*, is derived. It was long understood that only the return of God to save would bring Israel back from the deeper, spiritual exile of sinfulness, guilt and judgment (cf. Ezra 9:9; Neh. 9:36). And so the God Who has been with His people from the beginning now comes to be 'with them' in the climactic and unforgettable way of incarnation.

We are now in a position to take a long view of Joseph and ask: What is it that sums him up? We won't be far wrong when we describe him – as we did his wife, Mary – as a prototype disciple. The heartbeat of Christian discipleship is that of obedience. And the pattern of Joseph's obedience is transparently clear. In the first place, 'An angel … said: "Do not fear to take Mary [as] your wife' (Matt. 1:20, RSV). When Joseph awoke he promptly did as the angel had commanded him, and took Mary home as his wife (Matt. 1:24). Again, 'an angel of the Lord … said, "Get up … take … escape to Egypt" … So he got up, took the child and his mother' (Matt. 2:13,14). Third, 'an angel … said, "Get up … go to Israel" … So he got up, took the child and his mother and went' (Matt. 2:19–21).

In each instance Matthew wants his readers to know that these acts of obedience are but further evidences of the fulfilment of the prophetic scriptures – the latter, for Matthew, being the key to his 'infancy narratives'. We should add that his characteristic themes of righteousness and discipleship are also highlighted in Joseph's story. By focusing on Joseph's prompt obedience to divine instruction, Matthew seems to be illustrating, quite deliberately, what a just or righteous man is (Matt. 1:19). For the evangelist, Joseph is an early prototype disciple: the just person who lives by obedient faith. In short, a model believer.

As we have seen already, Joseph – the man who has to face up to a miracle, and one that is happening to someone else as well – is actually peripheral to the unfolding cosmic drama. Yet every act of obedience, even at the margins of the story, contributes significantly to its unfolding. An unrealistic faith is tempted to claim too much, and verges on idolatry when it tries to fit God into a world of its own making, with God as talisman to bless and prosper what we have planned. Authentic faith is entirely different. It lets God fit us into His big world and big plans, with all the attendant risks.

Cosy securities are thus cast adrift on the sea of faith; cosseted self-esteem is laid on the altar of mature self-sacrifice; careful futures are flung to the wind of His Spirit. 'In making disciples', said P.T. Forsyth, 'Christ ruined many careers.' For God is not here to be used. As Austin Farrer said, He is not 'a medicine in our cupboard nor a weapon in our armoury'.[4] Nor, we might add, is He a tool in our own little toolbox – because He will ultimately refuse to help us build our own house, preferring instead, if we will, to let us help Him build *his*.

COSTLY OBEDIENCE

Joseph exemplifies this costly obedience or, shall we say, inconvenient obedience. It is one thing to applaud God's providence; quite another to approve God moving in mysterious ways, especially when it affects us directly and we become one of those ways. For Joseph it must have meant sly looks, crude innuendo, aspersions cast about his son's legitimacy, coarse jokes at his expense in local taverns. It entailed leaving the business for relatives to manage while he took care of his heavily pregnant wife-to-be on the slow, bumpy trek south to Bethlehem for the Roman census. We can imagine his deep anxiety about the overcrowded inns, perhaps driving them to seek lodging with distant relatives more obligated than understanding. Then came the wonder of the birth, the ebullient shepherds bursting in breathlessly with the afterglow of glory on their weather-beaten faces.

Perhaps strangest of all was the long, long migration out of the shadow of impending death, Immanuel with them, to a land – Egypt – whose very mention evoked strong, conflicting emotions in the folk memories of his people. Should any of his old Nazareth workmates have made it to Egypt and asked him why he was there, we can perhaps imagine Joseph proudly replying: 'I must be about my son's business.'

CHAPTER EIGHT

The Aerial View

Read Luke 2:1–20

It is a book intended for the lounge rather than the study, but is enjoyable none the less. Titled *Britain: An Aerial Close-Up*, it was a Christmas present from friends. It is one of those lavish, coffee-table productions and contains a collection of stunning aerial photographs of the British landscape. It goes without saying that an aerial view shows you what you'd never see from ground level. Aerial photography gives you a new pair of eyes to see things from above, to see things in a new light, to see things in new perspective.

This is essentially what is happening to the shepherds in Luke's narrative. Angelic messengers from that other dimension of reality break in on the boring routine of their night shift. A glorious light dazzlingly illuminates the whole scene. They are scared witless at first! We can get so used to living in a tiny circle of light, lit by the candle of our own viewpoint or huddled round the campfire of our own daily routine. Suddenly the darkness that shuts us into smaller visions of ourselves is driven back; scarily the darkness that has shrunk the scale of our human identity is dispelled and we wake up to what too often we are unaware of – the fact that we are actors on a larger stage, players in a bigger picture. We wake up to a larger world; we wake up to realising we cannot define ourselves by our work; we wake up to a God of glory Who loves each one of us as infinitely valuable.

Bethlehem needs this aerial view of things. Bethlehem is full of tired people; people who've worked hard; people in overcrowded accommodation, having to share living space with unwelcome guests; people anxious about the changes disturbing their usual routine; people with financial worries, about how to make ends meet or fill in tax returns or balance the company books; people in need of a holiday.

One of my favourite Christmas cards is produced by Tearfund (The Evangelical Alliance Relief Agency). It depicts the shepherds on the hillside outside Bethlehem. One sheep is prodding one of the shepherds awake with one hoof; with another he is pointing to the glory rising behind him and the angels gathering at the back of the hill. The bleary-eyed shepherd says only: *'This had better be good!'*

And good it was!

- Glory does good; it makes all the difference.
- Glory comes only from God.
- Glory transfigures what is mundane and unexceptional.
- Glory is the aerial view of our human landscape.
- Glory sheds God's light on everything.
- Glory floods our lives with God's perspective.

I was brought up on J.B. Phillips' modern translation of the New Testament and was gripped by his version of Paul's prayer for the Colossian Christians: 'I pray that you may see things – as it were – from God's point of view.' The glory of Christmas gives us, as it were, a little aerial photography and invites us to see everything from God's point of view.

What particularly struck me as I leafed through the aerial photographs of Britain is that the view from the air inevitably highlights the most prominent feature of the landscape, be it a power station or a stately home. I noticed this. So many of our most famous towns would be unremarkable if it were not for the cathedrals that are their most prominent feature; Ely, for example.

Luke's aerial view of Bethlehem leaves the shepherds and us in no doubt as to the most prominent feature of that landscape (Luke 2:10–12). God's glory floods our world with light, and fearfully and wonderingly we awake to a wholly new perspective on everything. But even more remarkably, God's glory is focused in a baby being born – a king without a palace – a Saviour Who is Messiah of Israel and Lord of the world. Of course it's not easy to see this from ground level. The secret is to see things from God's point of view.

The secret is to approach the guest room of an overcrowded house – with no brass nameplate on the door, down a dark alley, off the beaten track of VIP traffic, in an unpretentious, small, country town in a back-of-beyond part of the world. It's a place you'd never visit unless you'd seen it from the air and from an angel's vantage point and unless, for a moment, the glory of heaven had lit up the landscape.

J.B. Phillips tells in his well-known little fable of how, once upon a time, a very young angel was being shown round the splendours and glories of the universe by a senior and experienced angel. To tell the truth, the little angel was getting tired and a little bored. He had been shown whirling galaxies and blazing suns, infinite distances in the deathly cold of interstellar space, and to his mind there seemed to be an awful lot of it. Finally he was shown the galaxy of which our planetary system is but a small part. The senior angel pointed to a small, insignificant sphere turning very slowly on its axis. It looked as dull as a dirty tennis ball to the little angel, compared to the size and glory of what he had seen.

> 'What's special about that one?'
> 'That'– replied the senior angel, solemnly – 'that is the visited planet.'
>
> 'Visited?' spluttered the junior angel.'You don't mean visited by …?'
>
> 'Indeed I do. That ball, which no doubt looks to you small and insignificant … has been visited by our young Prince of Glory.' And at these words he bowed his head reverently.[1]

As the angels tell the shepherds, the most prominent feature of our landscape is Jesus. From ground level it's not easy to see this; but the view from the air makes all the difference. When you see things from God's point of view it's absolutely clear. Glory to God in the highest is focused uniquely in Jesus. God's peace is for us on earth and it too is found only in Jesus.

> Our peace is his glory; His highest glory is our deepest joy.
>
> It is in our best self-interest that He gets glory for His

> getting glory and our finding salvation and satisfaction in Him converge.
>
> To seek His glory and our happiness is one and the same goal.[2]

When you see things from this vantage point there's only one thing you can do: get to Jesus as quickly as possible, verify the truth and believe in Him with every ounce of faith you've got.

Aerial photography – I reflect – is used in making maps. The aerial view makes clear a new direction for living. Just as glory comes from God to flood our lives with a new *perspective*; just as God's glory picks out Jesus as the most *prominent* feature of our lives, so glory flows back to God in people whose overriding *priority* is to live to the praise of His glory.

The shepherds returned to their work with a new sense of direction, 'glorifying and praising God for all the things they had heard and seen'. This was now their overwhelming new priority; to live to the praise and glory of God.

The secret of living at ground level is to retain as vivid a memory as you can of the glory of Christmas – that glimpse of the glory of God which by the Spirit you have seen in the face of Jesus Christ, and heard in the good news of His cross and resurrection.

The secret of earthly living as believers is to do all for the glory of God. I work for an inter-church Christian organisation, but our Christian witness does not consist merely in the content of our products or lectures. If we can grapple with financial spreadsheets, or computer graphics; if we can meet production deadlines, wrestle with management flow charts, devise marketing strategies, as well as teach the Bible, train counsellors, preach the gospel and conduct leadership seminars *to the glory of God* then we are a Christian organisation. We are, we have to remind ourselves, a Christian organisation, but only in so far as we maintain our Godward direction and our God-glorifying priority. Only if we retain and relish this reason for living will any of us have the stamina to go back to our work and face the future with confidence.

I recall being in Missouri, North India – a small town 8,000 feet up in the foothills of the Himalayas. 'Get up before dawn,' my friend said, 'and go round to the back of the hill.' We did and as we looked we saw the rising sun, out of sight beyond our hill, glinting on the snow-capped peaks of the world's highest mountains over 100 miles away. What a sight!

The future is obscure. We don't yet see the dawn of God's final day ahead of us. But as we look back to the first Christmas and Easter – to what seems a long way away from us – we see the rising sun bathing the snow-capped peaks in the morning glory of God's coming kingdom. Then we know we have a reason for living. My prayer for anyone pondering these meditations is that you may see things again from God's point of view and both taste the grace and glimpse the glory.

CHAPTER NINE

Glory in the Night

Read Luke 2:1–4, 8–18

The aerial view of things, which Luke gives in his vivid panorama of the birth of Jesus, offers us much needed perspective. Although he paints in broad brushstrokes, his artistry sketches in some glaring contrasts, which are sharp and deliberate. The world of political and economic affairs is contrasted with what is happening in an obscure province of the Holy Roman Empire and an even more obscure small town called Bethlehem (Luke 2:1–4). The world rulers of imperial Rome with all their grandeur are juxtaposed with an unknown peasant couple – Mary and Joseph – who are at the other end of the social spectrum altogether.

Augustus, born Gaius Octavian (grandnephew and adopted son of Julius Caesar and designated his heir), was acclaimed ruler of the entire Roman Empire in 27 BC. He acquired quasi-divine status, as this inscription affirms: 'Divine Augustus Caesar: son of a god, imperator of land and sea, the benefactor and saviour of the whole world'. But Luke makes mention of him in connection with the birth of Jesus in order to highlight the universal impact and significance of Jesus, not of Augustus. From an edict issued from the city of Rome, the world centre of secular power, attention switches to the emergence of real Kingship in the city of David (Luke 2:4b).

The Davidic echoes have already been heard in Luke's story, connecting with the ancient promises of God's King coming to rule (Luke 1:27,32,35,78,79; also 2:4). And Jesus, like David, is to be born in

Bethlehem (cf. Micah 5:2). Luke is telling us that the seemingly all-embracing authority and plans of Augustus Caesar are subordinate to God's plans and purposes. As Joel Green points out: 'One may call this ironic, as if Rome is made unwittingly to serve a still greater sovereign. But it is also prophetic, for it reveals the provisional nature of even Roman rule.'[1]

Rome is relativised; a greater than Caesar is here.

Yet 'there was no room for them in the inn' (Luke 2:7). This last word means 'lodging house' (also Luke 9:12; 19:7); whereas the word for 'commercial inn' (Luke 10:34) is different – and anyhow was not likely to be found in Bethlehem since it was not on any main routes. So the best supposition is that Mary and Joseph stayed with friends or relatives who lived in the typical cave houses of peasant people. The normal arrangement was for the resident family to occupy the top part with their animals beneath them on the ground floor. On this occasion, because the upper living space was filled to capacity, Mary had to give birth among the animals and the newborn babe was laid in a feeding trough.

GLORIOUS NIGHT

We take note of another stark contrast: that between shepherds on the one hand and angels on the other. Shepherds were peasants, situated at the lower end of the social scale of power and prestige. It is striking that the divine revelation of glory is not made to the VIPs mentioned above, who were men of power and influence, but to those in a despised trade with zero-ratings on the *Who's Who* list. Angels ceaselessly attend God's glory and so, not unsurprisingly, turn up here as that glory is manifested. Glory is the outward manifestation of God's holiness and presence. As a good complexion is an outward sign of health, so glory is the radiant, outward sign of God's holiness. Not surprisingly the shepherds – enveloped in the dazzling, golden mist of God's glory – find it all disconcerting (Luke 2:9).

The remarkable contrast here is with the Temple in Jerusalem (whose importance Luke has already noted). The Temple was the guaranteed meeting point of the heavenly and the earthly, the divine and the human. Both tabernacle and, later, Temple were flooded with the *shekinah* of God (cf. Exod. 40:35; 1 Kings 8:11). This appearance of the divine glory is remarkable precisely because the glory that is normally associated with the Temple is now manifest on a Judean hill farm. And what a contrast: the darkness of the 'night' (Luke 2:8c) and the luminous brilliance of 'the glory of the Lord [which] shone around them' (Luke 2:9). Joel Green again observes, 'This is the language of epiphany, the visible manifestation of the power of God certifying the presence of God in the coming of this child.'[2] Abraham, upon seeing God's glory; Moses' experience at the burning bush; Solomon overwhelmed by the glory cloud flooding the Temple; Isaiah caught in the penetrating, laser-like beam of God's holiness – none of them saw anything compared to this. For God is never more glorious than when He reveals Himself in Jesus of Nazareth.

GOOD NEWS

'The baby's born' … 'The rescue team is here' … 'The war is over'. The brevity of a soundbite suffices to tell this good news (Luke 2:10).

The baby's born: 'to you is born this day', a special child in the town where Israel's greatest kings came from and the good news is the arrival of *the Lord Jesus*. What is given is not another religion but Jesus Himself. The first-century world was awash with religions: astrological ones, occultic, spiritistic and immoral ones with prostitutes as sacraments, sensual ones that drenched initiates in bulls' blood, mystic ones fortified by drugs, intellectual ones touted by wandering sages and cynical philosophers. And Judaism, the truest religion the world has ever seen, was itself giving birth to the One Who is better than the best religion. While the initial manifestations of glory were eventually switched off, the radiance shone on in His face (John 1:14ff.; 2 Cor. 4:5,6), which is surely the best news of all.

The rescuers have arrived … we're safe. His is a rescue mission, to save us from our sins. It is this that makes Him 'Saviour'. Because of Him, 'hostages' are freed from their captivity; 'potholers' are lifted from their deep pit of despair.

The war is over … peace has broken out. The joyful news is trumpeted of 'sins forgiven, hell subdued and peace with heaven' (Isaac Watts), of 'God and sinners reconciled' (Charles Wesley). It needs pointing out that when the angelic chorus sings of peace between God and heaven and men on earth, it is not saying that there is goodwill towards men in general (indicative of the Santa Claus god of 'Xmas' fame), nor 'to men of good will', nor 'among men of goodwill'. Such interpretations invite a sentimental view of Christmas in which everyone is nice to each other until normal service is resumed on Boxing Day – not unlike the famous truce in the trenches during World War One. No; it is peace to people 'on whom God's favour rests'. Such words speak of the gospel of the grace of God.

IMPORTANT EVENT

And such grace is centred on Jesus Himself. Here is specifically 'good news'; the news of a child born a Saviour Who is 'Christ' (Messiah) and 'Lord' (Luke 2:11). The use of the word 'gospel' (Greek *euangellion*) here is significant, first, because it corroborates Isaiah's witness: 'You who bring good tidings to Zion, go up on a high mountain. You who bring good tidings to Jerusalem, lift up your voice with a shout' (Isa. 40:9; see also 52:7ff.; 61:1ff.). Second, it resonates with the use of the word in Luke's day. In the Roman world an *euangellion* was an imperial battle victory issued to announce some important event such as the emperor's birthday. Joel Green has pointed out that 'the birthday of the god – in this case the Emperor – marked for the world the beginning of good tidings through his coming'.[3] And this was said of Augustus.

So the angel's message is: 'cast in the form of an Imperial proclamation affirming that Jesus, not the Emperor Augustus, was the Saviour and source of peace, whose birthday, "this day", marked a new beginning of time'.[4]

The word 'saviour' (Greek *soter*) in Roman ears referred to only one person: the emperor himself, the giver of the *Pax Romana* – the enforced peace of Rome. In Jewish ears, the word pointed to Yahweh Himself as the only Saviour of His people (cf. Luke 1: 46,47). And this is the One Who lives up to His name of 'Jeshua' by saving both His people and the world from their sins by being God-with-us. He is 'Christ' or 'Messiah', Israel's anointed Davidic king, the Great Deliverer destined, according to Psalm 2, to be the ruler of the whole world. He, not the emperor, is the time *kurios* (Lord). Luke records these politically threatening titles in anticipation of the Day of Pentecost when Peter declares: 'Therefore let all Israel be assured of this: God has made this Jesus, whom you crucified, both Lord and Christ' (Acts 2:36).

Not surprisingly the Jews, who already had a king, and the Gentiles, who already had an overlord, did not take kindly to this nonviolent *coup d'état*, this silent revolution from beneath. Thus is prepared the way for the crucifixion of Jesus and the persecution of the apostles (Luke 2:34). But the way is also prepared for Luke's vivid account in Acts, his second volume, of the proclamation of the good news in Jerusalem and to the ends of the earth: that 'Jesus Christ is Lord'.

GRACIOUS SIGN

What exactly is the sign announced by the angels (Luke 2:12)? For Luke it is the amazing humility, the extraordinary condescension that the incarnation represents in his story. The very ordinariness of it all makes it extraordinary: the glorious light is switched off; the angelic choir departs; no brass plate is affixed to the stable door; no red carpet or VIP treatment laid on. When the blazing glory has dimmed and the heavenly singing fades away, what are we left with? Just the insignificant significance of stable and manger. Sobering echoes of Isaiah resonate in the child in the manger, and suggest that He is in the right place among a people of Israel who are not themselves in the right place concerning God's will for them (Isa. 1:3). This Christ in the crib points to how they can be at the centre of Yahweh's will and plan for them.

Concerning the swaddling clothes, there is perhaps an intriguing allusion to the non-canonical Jewish book of Wisdom and to the infant King Solomon, the recipient of divine wisdom: 'I was nursed with care in swaddling clothes. For no king has had a different beginning of existence; there is for all one entrance into life and one way out' (Wisd. 7:4,5).

Of course, Luke's Jesus, as the repository of God's wisdom, proves the great exception to the rule. His swaddling clothes wrap a deeper wisdom yet to be revealed. For this is the saving paradox at the heart of the story. Heaven opens every transcendent window to let out its radiance and pulls out every stop to sound its angelic praise. And yet, in the words of

Helmut Thielicke, boldly proclaiming faith in a war-devastated Hamburg,

> This incursion of eternity which fulfils all hope and longing is concentrated at a single point, namely, where the child lies in its crib, where the love of God is so big that it gives itself in what is smallest, where the eternity of God is so mighty that it enters a feeble and despised body.[5]

GENUINE RESPONSE

Did the shepherds take it personally? They certainly did. When our mail falls on the mat are we not the first to ask: Is there anything for me? The message of the angel was certainly intended to be taken personally: 'Good news *for you* … joy *for you* … born *to you* … sign *for you* …' And the 'great rejoicing' replaced the 'great fear' (Luke 2:9,10; cf. John 16:20–22, my italics).

In Luke's shepherd narrative, we observe the sense of great urgency these rough, peasant countrymen felt: 'Let's go now' (Luke 2:16, NRSV). We also see how the shepherds made accurate confession about the Christ-child, without adding or subtracting from what they had been told (Luke 2:17). And they glorified and praised God upon returning for all they had seen and heard, of course. But perhaps there is an added reason. The sheep being tended outside Jerusalem were probably destined for sacrifice on the altar in the Temple. So what else can shepherds do when they have found God's choicest Lamb of all, other than give vent to their praises? For when angel voices from another realm sang to them 'Glory to God in the highest', it found its echo in the lowliest and happiest band of shepherds you can imagine. We can picture them staggering back to the hill farm, bleary-eyed and dazed in soul, arms around one another as if drunk on happiness … 'praising and giving God the glory for all they had seen and heard'. Certainly those sheep would never have heard the end of it. This kind of good news was enough to make a sheep volunteer for sacrifice.

CHAPTER TEN

The Messianic Secret

Read Luke 2:19,51

Like fine wine laid down to await its maturity, so the Messiah's secret is stored up within Mary's faith, until its time will come. Mary 'treasured' and 'pondered' these things in her heart (Luke 2:19,51). She did this presumably until she recounted these things to Luke at a later time. I wonder when and how she told Jesus.

The reactions to the Christmas story are as vivid as they are varied: angels are ecstatic, Magi overjoyed, Herod outraged, shepherds seriously happy, glorifying and praising God and amazing everyone to whom they tell their story. But Mary? In contrast Mary 'treasured up all these things'. This phrase 'treasured up' perhaps has distant echoes of Jacob entrusted with his youngest son, Joseph's, dreams, or Daniel, sealing up the strategic visions of the kingdom (Gen. 37:11; Dan. 7:28; 8:26; 12:4,9).

So now, crucially, the riches of divine disclosure are put into the safekeeping of the humble heart of this young woman. She guards the cherished deposit. Like a jeweller appreciating the worth of precious stones, she turns these truths over in her mind and ponders them in her heart (Luke 1:19).

And 'ponder' she might, for the mystery of divine revelation invites attempts at penetrating its significance, something which she no doubt continued to do for the next thirty years. So it is that Mary is entrusted with both the baby and the secret of His significance.

Just as Luke intends the shepherds' enthusiastic

blazoning abroad of the message to inspire our own open testimony to the newborn Jesus so, too, he intends Mary's 'treasuring and pondering' to turn us to inner reflection and contemplation on the whole mystery of the incarnation. So by pondering the heart of the story (Luke 2:14–20), we pause to reflect on the rich theology of Christmas, the priceless treasure of the Incarnation.

THE PRIORITY OF CHRISTMAS: GOD'S GLORY

There is here an order of things. First, God's glory, then our peace. This is the angelic sense of priority. When the angels appear on the hillside, 'glory' is the visible manifestation of the holy mystery of God. Here in the angels' song, 'glory' means the honour given to God. And the words 'in the highest' imply that all heaven is impressed by what God is doing on earth and that glory accrues to God in heaven because of what is happening here. The birth of Messiah, then, brings glory to God like nothing else before. 'Very God and very man', Christ is the final burning bush. 'We look,' reflected Austin Farrer,

> and we see a fire of divine glory, burning in a sweet flourishing tree, which is not consumed – that is, we see Jesus, a kind face of human flesh, in which the very godhead burns; and yet his common manhood is not destroyed.[1]

The arrival of Israel's Messiah and the world's Lord on His saving mission enhances God's reputation as nothing else does. Everything that occurs in the story tends to God's praise, as demonstrated by the participants. Angels, Magi and shepherds in their own ways glorify God in their worship and praise. In characteristically robust fashion, Martyn Lloyd-Jones underscores the crucial point here:

> The moment salvation is mentioned it is the glory of God that is most prominent ... As the chief element in our sin is that we do not give to God the glory due to his name, so the chief thing about salvation should be that it brings us a realisation of the glory of God.[2]

Emil Brunner concurs: 'In the Bible the glory of God is the first concern; the salvation of man comes second'.[3] There is no salvation, no peace until God and His glory are restored to their rightful place – at the centre of everything.

THE PROVISION OF CHRISTMAS: GOD'S PEACE

When Luke records 'and on earth peace' he is not envisaging either the absence of war, human conflict or inner tranquillity – some quiet state of the heart. What is meant is the peace of God's kingdom, the *shalom* or wholeness, well-being and justice of that kingdom. All of which is heralded by the prophets of old, such as Isaiah when he spoke of there being no end to the increase of God's government (Isa. 9:7). And the prophet's formative use of the concept of 'gospel' has as its central feature the proclamation of 'peace' (Isa. 52:7ff.). Here is the peace that characterises Messiah's rule and reign, the longed-for era of salvation.

Luke has already emphasised the worldwide impact of Jesus and the universal repercussions of His coming. And his Gospel traces the revolutionary upheaval that Jesus will cause in Israel, right up to the final showdown in Jerusalem. Then in the Acts of the Apostles, Luke takes the story of his Gospel on from Jerusalem to the very centre of power in Rome, with Paul continuing to teach the radical message of the kingdom.

But some might well ask: Wasn't the world already enjoying peace, the peace of the *Pax Romana*? Yes, indeed. But this latter peace was in reality a refined form of protection racket, a totalitarianism disguised as benevolent, which was efficiently administered yet militarily enforced. God's intrusive offer of peace on earth radically undermines the 'peace of Rome' and exposes it as deeply flawed.

So the peace of God announced that day was not a process, the result of compromise and careful negotiation. It was a peace that would be seen to lie on the other side of a fierce and final battle, a showdown with evil and the rebellious spiritual powers; a peace that would cost the lifeblood of this child. By His birth is 'our peace'; only by his death does he 'make the peace' effective (Eph. 2:14).

THE CLEAR DIRECTION OF CHRISTMAS: GOD'S GRACE TOWARDS US

The words 'men on whom his favour rests' indicate that God's favour and good pleasure rest on those caught up in God's achievement: in His glorifying and peacemaking in Christ. The movement is self-evidently downwards because this is always the direction of grace: from God to us, from heaven to earth, from the highest to the lowest. There is no question here of climbing a ladder to God but of God 'coming down to us'. Which is why in the last analysis we are less astonished by angels than they are astonished at God's condescending to save us sinners – a matter that commands their angelic interest and into which they 'long to look' (1 Pet. 1:12).

THE PARADOX OF CHRISTMAS, GOD'S VULNERABILITY

How unimaginable: God as a baby! Aptly and famously, Wesley sang of that mystery: 'Our God contracted to a span, Incomprehensibly made man.' Luke's repetition of the use of the word 'child' highlights both the humility of God and the seeming risk of the whole enterprise. Here is glory but obscured in a manger. Now is spoken worldwide peace but hidden in an obscure backwater of a town. This is the epicentre of God's power but wrapped up in the fragility of Jesus. Let us ponder these things until the power of paradox opens our eyes to the omnipotence of love, which breaks our proud strength by its startling weakness and subverts our mental defences by its sublime foolishness. To be humble is not to will less but to will more. Humility is not the path of least resistance but the royal road to victory.

'The great eternal act of Christ in heaven and Godhead, before and beyond history', said P.T. Forsyth,

> was of a like nature to the long act of will by which He went down to death in His human history. It was an act of heart and will, of free resolve, of self-limitation, self-contraction as it were, self-divesting, self-humiliation, self-subordination.[4]

The unreachable becomes the unmissable. In Robert Barron's words,

> The God Who is disclosed in the unheard of event of the Incarnation is One Who, in the most dramatic sense, cannot be grasped (for he controls the stars, the angels, and the most powerful forces in the world) and cannot be avoided (for he becomes in the humblest way one of us, stooping to the lowest position).[5]

If we look carefully we shall see that the sign on the cradle is the mark of the cross. As Austin Farrer again said, and once more in striking imagery,

> God will be loved whatever it may cost, and when he had expanded the flower of glory in his human life, he crushed it into a handful of petals for fear that power and wonder might stand between his kindness and our affections.[6]

CHAPTER ELEVEN

First Family

Read Luke 2:21; Mark 3:31–35; John 19:25–27

'The First Family' is how American Presidents style their households. The Clintons and the Bushes followed this tradition with Hillary Clinton and then Laura Bush each quickly establishing herself as First Lady in the 'First Family'. 'Family First' has become something of a slogan of politicians ready to capitalise on the breakdown of domestic order and anxious to promote family values.

In Britain, Chief Rabbi Jonathan Sacks, in his perceptive and typically Jewish insight into contemporary culture, urges a recovery of family life as the key to a successful society.[1] With dysfunctional families all around us – to say nothing of perhaps our own familial experience of pain – no one will doubt the wisdom of all this. The more telling, then, is Luke's note that on returning to Nazareth with Mary and Joseph, Jesus 'was obedient to them' (Luke 2:51). That Jesus was also content to live in an obscure Nazareth-based family where His Messiahship would be nurtured, is very instructive. During His ministry He clearly reaffirmed the family. He condemned quick and easy divorce; he welcomed children eagerly and lovingly; he spoke sharply in defence of widows; he criticised social and even religious practices that damaged family life and care.

Yet Luke also tells us about an incident from Jesus' growing years – in fact the only one on record – that frightens and angers His parents, as He quite unselfconsciously affirms His higher loyalty to His heavenly

Father's house (Luke 2:49,50). Clearly making an idol of the family is not the best way either to serve or to save it. For as much as Jesus reaffirmed the family, He also revolutionised family life as He knew it, just as He revolutionised everything in Israel. Rodney Clapp's book, *Families at the Crossroads*, is a stimulating exception to the usual Christian mantra on the subject. In it Clapp argues provocatively that Jesus subverted traditional Jewish allegiances. 'There can be no doubt', he writes, 'that Jesus displaced the biological family. For those who would follow him, family could no longer be paramount in the service of God'.[2] Of course, no one was better placed to evaluate this assertion than Jesus' own mother. Her story is one of family life turned inside-out by the upside-down kingdom of God that Her son had come to establish. We need to examine that story in some detail to do it justice.

INVADED BY GRACE

Mary's story begins with the quiet serenity of her life being shattered by the phenomenon of an angelic visitation. Then as a young girl engaged to be married she is invaded by God's grace (Luke 1:26–28). Mary was clearly shaken by the angel's news and thrown into a state of great agitation, her mind in turmoil with the possible implications of this greeting (Luke 1:29). Suddenly, her life seems to be spinning out of control. For her, certainly, it will never be the same again. She has been 'bothered by perfection'.[3] The gift of Jesus changed everything, upsetting all her plans, cancelling the hope of a quiet wedding.

And what about Joseph; will he disown her? Will her friends scorn her? Would there be talk of stoning her as an alleged adulteress? Out of the blue, grace shatters all her dreams. Her preconceived ideas about how her life will work out now lie in shreds. The hoped-for steady, unspectacular but satisfying routine as a carpenter's wife – respected and liked in an unpretentious village community – has gone for ever.

A GREAT CHALLENGE

Whatever her immediate reaction, however, Mary's settled response, as we have noted, is both moving and instructive: 'May it be to me as you have said' (Luke 1:38). There and then she starts to confront the great challenge posed for her by the coming of her son: should she be His mother or His disciple? Her Spirit-filled cousin Elizabeth has no doubt that the die is cast: 'Blessed is she who has believed that what the Lord has said to her will be accomplished!' (Luke 1:45). For her, Mary's faithful, obedient and humble acceptance of the gift of grace opens her to a life of blessing. Much later, in the ministry of Jesus, when someone offers a piece of 'soundbite theology' about being blessed (Luke 11:27,28), He brings such sentimentality down to earth by declaring, 'Blessed rather are those who hear the word of God and obey it.' Just as His mother did.

UNFORGETTABLE NIGHT

How blessed she was that night of the birth. She would never forget it: unkempt shepherds staggering in like drunken men, wide-eyed with wonder, almost incomprehensible in telling what they had seen and heard. Gushingly they tell her about the glorious light they had seen and the ethereal song they had heard, whose lyrics were mysterious to them and whose melody for ever eluded them when they tried to repeat it. For her part Mary did what must be done with unspeakable joy and glimpses of unimaginable glory; she locked up such secrets in her memory bank and buried the priceless treasure of the song deep within her (Luke 2:19).

And perhaps once in a while, as she watched and waited during those long, growing years, she took the memories out and pondered their value and significance. Already she sensed that the coming of Jesus into her life had planted a seed of divine discontent that would leave her profoundly dissatisfied and unable to rest until she had seen this stage through to its conclusion; unable to settle for anything less than to see that glory and to sing that song herself.

MEANINGFUL PRESENTATION

We next see Mary as the proud and glowing mother of a six-week-old baby, bringing Him to Jerusalem for presentation as her first-born at the Temple (Luke 2:22–24). 'But when the time had fully come,' Paul wrote to the Galatians, 'God sent his Son, born of a woman, born under law, to redeem those under law, that we might receive the full rights of sons' (Gal. 4:4,5). What Paul paints on a big canvas, Luke picks out in detail: 'On the eighth day, when it was time to circumcise him, he was named Jesus ... When the time of their purification according to the Law of Moses had been completed, Joseph and Mary took him to Jerusalem to present him to the Lord' (Luke 2:21). But the evangelist, like Paul, wants to emphasise both Jesus' full immersion in our humanity ('born of woman') and his full submission to the law of God ('born under law'). Both dimensions, Luke sees, are integral to the redemption that comes with Jesus. Let's now take a closer look at these twin features in turn.

First, Jesus' full submission to the law ('under the law'). Luke goes to some lengths to emphasise this fact: 'according to the Law of Moses' (Luke 2:22); 'as it is written in the Law of the Lord' (Luke 2:23); 'in keeping with what is said in the Law of the Lord' (Luke 2:24); 'everything required by the Law of the Lord' (Luke 2:39). Circumcision, which was the seal of covenant membership, marks Jesus out as someone fully identified with God's purposes for all the sons of Abraham (Gen. 17:9–14; Lev. 12:3). It graphically foreshadows that greater and more drastic circumcision, the 'stripping off of his flesh' in crucifixion.

The presentation of the baby Jesus at the Temple places Him, as the pre-eminent first-born, at the forefront of personal dedication to Yahweh and to His service (see Exod. 13). The offerings that His parents brought were the poorest allowable gifts and yet herald His self-offering to the Father for the sake of all. And the act of purification for His parents but especially Mary His mother, lines Jesus up with the required purity that God expects (see Lev. 12).

LARGER SIGNIFICANCE

These details of how Jesus is brought 'under the law' point to the larger significance of what is going on. For in submitting to the law in these particular details, Jesus, even as a baby, is embarking on the road of redemption. On behalf of us all, He will both fulfil the law's obligations as well as bear the law's penalties. By doing this from birth unto death, He will redeem us all and enable us to live not 'under law' but under grace, not by the natural order of things but by the Spirit of God. So it is that the details in this infancy narrative speak of Jesus' central significance for the outworking of God's great saving purposes, as disclosed in Scripture.

The first two chapters of Luke's account have been described as a veritable 'echo chamber' of Old Testament stories and promises, from Abraham and Israel through to kings and prophets. As we have already seen, Luke sees the birth of John and Jesus through the 'window' of Samuel and the emergence of kingship in Israel. So the presentation of Jesus reflects the presentation of Samuel (see 1 Sam. 1:11,21–28). Overtones of Isaiah's visions and prophetic promises (Isa. 8; 9; 40–55) are scattered everywhere too.

In other words, in submitting to the law, Jesus is not

simply conforming in an ad hoc way to an occasional requirement of the law. Something much bigger in scale is happening. He is absorbing into His own life and mission the covenant vocation of Israel – and beyond that the long-range, redemptive purposes of God. The time for all of this had now fully and finally arrived.

The second feature is Jesus' full immersion in the human family ('born of a woman'). All the participants in Luke's infancy narrative – Zechariah and Elizabeth, Simeon and Anna and, not least, his parents Mary and Joseph – are willing supporters of God's aim. By placing Jesus within a law-abiding, God-loving family, Luke, narratively speaking, places Jesus at the centre of God's saving will and purpose. With them He is shaped for His mission.

A STUNNING PRONOUNCEMENT

While in Jerusalem, Mary hears from a faithful priest, Simeon, a stunning pronouncement and a sombre, painful prophecy: 'A light for revelation to the Gentiles and for glory to your people Israel ... And a sword will pierce your own soul too' (Luke 2:32–35). Her boy was to be the light of the world and the glory of Israel, but not without causing disturbance and division, not without bringing out the worst as well as the best in people; not without becoming a target for fierce enemies. All of which she would feel herself, like a sword thrusting through her own heart.

THE GROWING YEARS

But for now it's back to Nazareth and the years of the boy's childhood (Luke 2:41ff.). It was on the return journey from the feast of Passover in Jerusalem that Mary and Joseph realised that Jesus was not with them. 'Help!' … 'Where is he?'… 'He's not here!'… panic stations! And anger (Luke 2:48). Jesus' reply is baffling, hurtful, threatening and to the effect that He has bigger business to attend to, business that will cause Him to outgrow the domestic circle His mother prizes so highly. He will not forever be able to fit into her small, parochial world, as she has yet to discover. She will have to fit into His. Even at twelve years of age, Jesus appears to be moving in larger orbits than His parents could ever contemplate (Luke 2:46–47). Here are more jewels to store away in the archives of Mary's memory, kept in her safe-deposit box of unexplained mysteries. For the next eighteen years, life goes on predictably enough, with the children growing up, and Mary's strong, capable eldest son, taking up His father's trade of carpenter. One day, however, He takes leave of absence.

Calvin Miller has memorably pictured the young man from Galilee who hears the one, true Song of the great Earthmaker. Knowing that he alone has been called to sing to save the world, he smashes his mallet on the vice fixed to the carpentry bench and sets off as the singer of the Song. At the Jordan River he hears the Song again and learns to call the great Earthmaker, 'Father-Spirit'. At once he confronts the World Hater who plays an alternative melody. But the singer refuses to dance to his tune or turn aside from singing the true Song. So he returns home to take leave of his mother:

> 'MOTHER, I AM THE SINGER' He blurted out at once. 'I know' she said, 'I heard the Ancient Star-Song only once. It was the very night you were born. And all these years, my son, I've known you would come to board the shop some day. Can you sing the Star-Song yet?'
>
> 'I can,' he answered back.
>
> 'You know the final verse?' his mother asked.
>
> 'I know it all,' he answered back. 'But I'll not sing it here. I'll wait till I am on the wall … God give me strength to sing upon the wall – the Great Walled City of the Ancient King.' He turned.
>
> She cried, 'Leave off the final verse and not upon the wall.'
>
> He kissed her. 'I can't ignore the Father-Spirit's call
> So I will sing it there and I will sing it all.'[4]

INCREASINGLY HIS DISCIPLE

With their mockery and malice, many voices tried to drown out the Song the singer sang. It was when they began to say He was mad (Mark 3:21) that Mary felt, like all good mothers would, that she had to intervene to protect her son and His reputation. Was Jesus' perhaps surprising response a reproof to her maternal attempts to control the situation? His radical restatement of who constitute His true family must have cut deep: 'Whoever does God's will is my brother and sister and mother' (Mark 3:35). At which point she must have felt an 'outsider' in every respect. Even at a family wedding when she suggested He help after the wine had run out, He spoke to her in words bordering on disrespect: 'Dear woman, why do you involve me? ... My time has not yet come' (John 2:4ff.). Yet from somewhere she felt the stirring of a deep secret beneath the rejection and blurted out 'Do whatever he tells you'. Mary heard her son 'sing the Song'; it wove its magic over her too. And it became increasingly compelling so that she felt less and less His mother and more and more His disciple.

But she had always known there was a final verse to be sung: 'You know the final verse.' At last her dilemma is resolved. Life with her son Jesus, was for her, as it is for us, an unfolding mystery. Glimpses of divine glory dazzle us into an adventure with Him. The gift of grace that Jesus gives to us changes our lives irrevocably, disrupts our plans and dreams and gives us bigger ones. All this finds its focus at the foot of the cross. Will she be only His mother or will she be His disciple too? The issue is resolved:

> When Jesus saw his mother there, and the disciple whom he loved standing near by, he said to his mother, 'Dear woman, here is your son,' and to the disciple, 'Here is your mother.' From that time on, this disciple took her into his home.
>
> John 19:26,27

Now she finds her true identity as a disciple of her son

and thus finds a new Son. She receives new honour as a member of His embryonic family, the Church, which is just where we find her in the early days of the Church (Acts 1:14). And so it is that Mary can say 'First Family' – yes: *first His family, then her own.*

There can be no doubting that we would love our children better by loving Jesus more. Catholics, Protestants and Orthodox still fight over Mary, over her significance, her value. She remains a controversial figure: Mother of Jesus or Mother of God? I suggest she is 'First Lady' precisely because she was first His disciple, and second His mother. For me Mary will always be the 'First Lady' in the Family of Faith.

Father of the Great Family, I pray that all who share these reflections may be intruded upon by reality, inconvenienced by the incarnation, embarrassed by your humility, invaded by your glory and inundated by your love. Like Mary, may we, in our measure, be blessedly 'bothered by perfection'.
Amen.

CHAPTER TWELVE

A Spirit-Stirred Man

Read Luke 2:22–32

I'm particularly fond of old people, especially God's old people. 'Just as well,' some of my friends will say, 'since we are all aging together.' But I'm thinking more of a dear friend of mine, Vera, who used to play the organ in the first church I pastored. When my wife and I last visited her in her sheltered accommodation, she wanted above all to tell us how good the Lord had been to her. She told us of a dream she had had as a small girl, in which she saw a path leading up to half-opened door. Peeping through, she saw Jesus, Who said to her: 'One day when you want to come through this door, I'll be here to welcome you.' Then Vera turned to us and said animatedly, with eyes sparkling and face aglow: 'I can't wait to give him a big hug!' We reckoned this a noble ambition in a lady who, at the time of our visit, was three weeks away from her one-hundred-and-first birthday.

I am tempted to say at this point that with friends like that who needs Bible characters. In fact friends like Vera can put you in mind of Bible characters – in this case *Simeon* (Luke 2:25–38). Simeon is described as 'righteous and devout' (Luke 2:25). Before we pass over these adjectives, it's worth pausing to reflect how odd such a description sounds to modern ears. Luke means it as a tribute but to contemporary taste it sounds suspiciously like 'dull and boring'.

Tradition has it that Simeon was an elderly man. If so, the first challenge older people like Simeon offer us is to be *faithful rather than fashionable.* One advantage of growing older is that we really don't have to try very hard to be unfashionable. It comes with the territory. As we shall see, to say this is not to endorse a reactionary reclusiveness that retreats into a past time-warp. Quite the contrary; no one is shown to be more 'up to speed' than Simeon. But it is to encourage us to keep up with God's times, not ours. Younger people inevitably find this harder. I remember how it was, wanting so much to be part of the pack. When you are young, you are frightened to be odd or eccentric. Peer pressure or cultural conformity can so easily blunt the cutting edge of kingdom distinctiveness.

If we wanted Luke to put a better spin on things, we might rewrite his narrative to describe Simeon as 'relevant and exciting' or 'rich and influential' or 'trendy and fun-loving' – anything but 'righteous and devout'. But it doesn't on the whole seem to fit. That's because 'righteous and devout' suit God better as hallmarks of His authentic covenant people. With them there is no hankering after a lost past but a hope for the future and an acute awareness of the eternal now. Simeon, like my friend Vera in her own measure, is still dreaming dreams of what God will do. Simeon was among those *'waiting' expectantly 'for the consolation of Israel'*.

If you've ever known anything of the Holy Spirit's presence and power in your life, you will know a deep, underlying discontent. It is a divine discontent, placed there by the Spirit to guard against complacency, boredom and apathy. As Von Hugel once put it: 'God has put salt in our mouths.' Instilled in us is a profound longing and dissatisfaction with anything less than God's best, weaning us off being totally replete with anything else. If you have been smitten in the past by the Spirit, you are never the same person again: memories tantalise, echoes resound, the fragrance hangs in the air, the melody lingers on, tastebuds once caressed by the finest vintage wine can never forget. When nothing really satisfies, it is time for God again.

Simeon is a great help here. He 'personifies faithful and expectant Israel'.[1] He stands as a true model of the Spirit-stirred believer.

THE HOLY SPIRIT WAS UPON HIM

The evidence for asserting that the Spirit was upon him (Luke 2:25) was that Simeon was 'waiting for the consolation of Israel', which was the Messianic Age of salvation. In particular, the prophet Isaiah describes the age in chapters 40–45 in his prophecy, highlighting such aspects as: 'comfort my people' (Isa. 40:1); 'restore the tribes of Jacob' (Isa. 49:6); and 'the Lord will surely comfort Zion' (Isa. 51:3). What challenges us is that Simeon was moved by the Spirit to look for something beyond himself, something bigger than his own needs, something larger than his own interests and concerns. He is not preoccupied with his own feelings and moods. Although an elderly man, he is not glaze-eyed with nostalgia, grumpy with cynicism or morbid with resignation. Instead he is alert and eager for all that God is planning to do. That can only be the work of the Holy Spirit.

Simeon gains early entry to the Pentecostal class of those who – young or old – 'dream dreams and see visions'; those who are still looking to the future with great expectation and hope. In such a frame of mind, 'God gave him power to understand the importance of what was happening at that moment in Israel's history.'[2]

IT HAD BEEN REVEALED TO HIM BY THE HOLY SPIRIT

We find that Simeon is open to the revelation that only the Holy Spirit can give, determined as he was that 'he would not die before he had seen the Lord's Christ' (Luke 2:26). From this we can deduce that Simeon is not blinded by the natural light of human reason, nor by what the experts were saying, nor by what was rationally obvious. He is not absorbed with what was preoccupying the news media of the day, the politics and power games of the high and mighty in the land. He is listening for another voice; marching to a different drumbeat. Nor is he limited by merely natural vision or mystic insight. No! *We find him open to a supernatural revelation of God's point of view*, to seeing things from God's angle of vision alone.

In the light of Simeon's perspectives, we might pose some relevant questions for ourselves: Does the Holy Spirit set my ambitions and goals? What is it I must do, I must achieve, or travel to, or see, before I die? Our answers will be a good guide as to how much we are living by the revelation of the Spirit. As Martyn Lloyd-Jones so typically put it:

> How do I keep myself going? What is it that enables me to live? Am I living in the hope that something wonderful is going to happen, and that all our troubles will be banished and all will be well in a year's time or two years, or perhaps ten years' time? Am I still clinging to something that is going to happen in this life and in this world for my happiness? If I am, then, according to the New Testament, I am worldly minded; I am carnally minded.[3]

HE WAS MOVED BY THE SPIRIT

The opening words of Luke 2:27 can also be rendered: 'He came in the Spirit' (Greek *en tou pneumati*), which certainly covers all the action described in verses 27–35. It is fascinating to see how God choreographs the whole scene. He leads Mary and Joseph through His Word as they follow the requirements of the Torah (Luke 2:27b). He guides Simeon through the Spirit to come to the Temple at just the right time. As Joel Green points out: 'The result of this choreography is this rendezvous.'[4] He goes on to say,

> This appointment is not the result of divine coercion. Although God is operative through the Law and the Spirit to achieve this end, this encounter is dependent on the obedience of these human actors, who by their actions are helpers or supporters of the divine purpose.[5]

So it is that Simeon is willing to be 'moved by the Spirit', to be 'guided by the Spirit' (Luke 2:27b, NRSV).

What does this indicate for us? That being 'in the Spirit' converts the ordinary into the extraordinary. We tend to be over-fascinated with extraordinary manifestations and sensational phenomena. But the Holy Spirit is most often at work in the ordinary and everyday affairs of living. It is in the middle of the mundane that He sets His 'traps' of extraordinary significance and import.

At this particular time in Simeon's story, the Spirit led him to perform well all his regular priestly duties. And he knew the reality of the Spirit working with him in the mundane routine of his daily responsibilities. The Spirit enabled him to recognise this particular child in his arms as the Messiah. The Spirit inspired him to sing the magnificent song that we call the *Nunc Dimittis* – so named in the Latin from its initial words in the Vulgate version of the Bible. Simeon can sign off with contentment: 'Let me like a watchman or sentry go off duty, Lord; for my eyes have seen your salvation.' Let's now go on to consider his song of praise in greater detail.

SPIRIT-INSPIRED SONG

Sovereign Lord, as you have promised,
you now dismiss your servant in peace.
For my eyes have seen your salvation,
which you have prepared in the sight of all people,

> a light for revelation to the Gentiles
> and for glory to your people Israel.
>
> Luke 2:29–32

At one level this Song expresses profound personal satisfaction: Simeon sings of a long-held dream come true. Just as in the Genesis account Jacob found peace in gazing on the face of Joseph (Gen. 46:30), so Simeon finds deep fulfilment in looking on the face of Jesus Messiah. At a deeper level, Simeon represents God's people, Israel, which at last has found the final reason for its existence in the coming of its Messiah and King.

Yet Jesus is not only Yahweh's salvation for Simeon and for Israel; at the same time He is salvation for the world. And this salvation, which Jesus embodies, has been prepared 'in the sight of all people' (Luke 2:31). In this phrase we catch echoes of Old Testament Scripture, particularly of Isaiah: 'The Lord will bare his holy arm in the sight of all nations' (Isa. 52:10); and the psalmist: 'The Lord has made his salvation known … to the nations' (Psa. 98:2).

PROPHETIC PERSPECTIVE

Simeon praises God with far-reaching prophetic perspective. Jesus is the Light revealing God to all the Gentile nations, in fulfilment of the promise made to Abraham (Gen. 12:3). Jesus is that light of saving revelation to the whole world, reaffirmed as the prophetic hope by Isaiah (Isa. 42:6; 49:6; 60:1ff.). In short: Jesus is the only true Light of the world. But Jesus is also the very glory of God in and for Israel. That very radiance once reflected, dazzlingly, on the face of Moses; that same radiance, once pervasive in the Temple like a fine, golden mist, is now concentrated in this human form. 'The Word became flesh and ... We have seen his glory' (John 1:14). 'Jesus is God's final and decisive revelation to Israel. In and through him Israel can reach its ultimate goal as the people of God. Therefore Jesus is called its "glory".'[6]

In summary we can say that Jesus embodies the vocation of Israel to be a light to the nations, and replaces the Temple as the focal point in Israel of God's glory on earth.

TWO REFLECTIONS

The ground we have just surveyed concerning Simeon's Song suggests two possible contemporary reflections. The first is: Will 'revival' come? History tells us that revival usually begins through a small group of saints. They are devout and righteous, unsatisfied with what they see in their own lives and stirred by a divine discontent about the Church. Such people are not locked up in their own affairs and concerns; they are less absorbed in their own interests and more absorbed in God's purposes, God's people and God's world. Such people are not paralysed by the disappointments or successes of the past but are still looking forward with great expectation to what God might do, could do, and may want to do among them.

Without doubt the Holy Spirit can initiate great things and mighty movements by people who remain steadfast. In their praying, in their faithfulness, in their expectancy, in their sensitivity to every nuance of the Spirit, it is just such an authentic people of God who form the 'welcoming committee' for Jesus. To people like this God originally entrusted redemption; to people like this in our own day he might just entrust revival.

The second reflection is this: if Simeon is anything to go by, then Jesus is enough.

Some think He is, be it Charles Wesley – 'Thou, O Christ, art all I want; More than all in Thee I find' or the contemporary troubadour, Michael Card: 'Now that I have held him in my arms; My life can come to an end'.[7] Is He enough? I ask myself the question. Would it be enough just to have held Him for a fleeting moment in one's arms? Will my friend Vera's hug of relief be enough to make the long living and long waiting worthwhile? To have seen Him, known Him, held Him in the arms of our hearts, will this be enough to make dying a pathway to peace? The Puritan writer Richard Stibbes commented: 'Christ himself is nothing else but salvation clothed in our flesh … When we embrace Christ in the arms of faith, we embrace nothing but salvation.' And Matthew Henry offered his own supportive words: 'The consolation of Israel is to be waited for and it is worth waiting for, and it will be very welcome to those who have waited for it, and continue waiting.'

Isn't the world still waiting, like Dickens' Mr

Macawber, for 'something to turn up', for their luck to change, for their lottery number to come up? Or do some wait perhaps – as the two morbid tramps did in Samuel Beckett's acclaimed drama (or rather non-drama) *Waiting for Godot* – in existential resignation that the One Who gives meaning to living will never turn up?

But aren't we, His disciples, still waiting? Yes, we are, for the Saviour of the world and in the blessed hope of His second appearing. Yet what a difference there is between those who wait for a dream to come true and those who wait because their dream has already come true, taken flesh and dwelt among them; between those waiting for something to turn up and those waiting for Someone to return, Someone Who has been here already, Who promises to come back, and the integrity of Whose vows and deeds enables us to trust Him for His ultimate promise to be kept. What a difference there is between waiting with resignation because life is pointless, and waiting with eager expectation for the One Who makes life worthwhile; between waiting for grim death, and living and dying in hope of the resurrection of the body and the life eternal. We can say truly that:

He is salvation;
He is the Glory of God for Israel;
He is the God-revealing Light of the world;
He is the sweetest satisfaction for living;
He is the greatest prize for dying;
He is the deepest peace for every heart!

Depart with Him and we don't leave empty, we leave full. And we never know; by the mercy of the Spirit of God we, who hold Him in our hearts as salvation and glory, light and peace, might yet see with our own eyes the great revival that God has prepared to be poured out in the sight of all people. To see that would be to die happy!

CHAPTER THIRTEEN

Prophetic Sign, Painful Sword

Read Luke 2:33–38

Have we a vision for the Church at the beginning of the new millennium? I reflect on the amount of time I have spent in my church-life promoting major 'visions', inspired as we were by the challenge of Israel's sage who said: 'Where there is no prophetic vision the people cast off restraint' (Prov. 29:18, ESV). Somewhat ruefully, I now think that it's become more fashionable for the Church to talk about its vision than about its mission. This is a sign of the times. Businesses used to draw up their mission statements, in which they outlined their company's aims and objectives. Now they are as likely to spend time, money and creative energy drawing up their vision statements – which are surely mission statements in fancy dress!

Social commentator John Morrish has observed: 'Once upon a time someone who admitted to a "vision" was either an Old Testament prophet, a religious mystic or mad. Nowadays, he's more likely to be a Management Consultant.'[1]

He continues:

> Every modern, go-ahead organisation now has a 'vision' expressed in something called a Vision Statement – which often disguises the true work of the company. Whereas the Mission Statement addresses harsh realities, the Vision Statement is about values. So while your Vision Statement might declare: 'Our aim is to achieve world peace' your Mission Statement would be forced to admit: 'We supply heavy artillery to the world's emerging countries!'[2]

Which begs the question: Must the vision statement always cunningly disguise the real mission objective? Again Simeon comes to our aid. He does so especially with his Spirit-inspired Song and prophetic statement (Luke 2:29–32), made over the baby Jesus and His mother, in which he sings of the people's expectations and God's preparation.

GREAT EXPECTATIONS

Expectancy was in the air. Such expectancy was shared by the faithful in Israel, such as Simeon and Anna the prophetess. They were 'looking for the consolation of Israel', for an end to Israel's long exile from God's favour, and anticipating the long-awaited day of forgiveness and grace (Luke 2:25,38). Other Jews at the time were also longing for an end to oppression by Rome's pagan power; longing for politico-economic freedom again through a new exodus, longing for the people's liberation from their grinding poverty and humiliation.

Beyond the confines of Israel, in the wider, Gentile world, the search for the light of revelation was widespread and intense. Archeologists have unearthed many inscriptions in the ancient world that describe prayers, pleas and potions that invoke 'salvation' for the people. Other means were used, such as magic, the occult, the deification – as we have already noted – of the Emperor Augustus (hailed by many as *soter*, saviour, and prince of peace); mystery religions involving bloody initiation rites with weird, sexually depraved cultic rituals. Then on a higher plane altogether was the ongoing search by the intellectual elite, the philosophers and sages.

Michael Green asserts in summary that

> at the time of Jesus' birth, there was a deep longing for salvation throughout the length and breadth of the ancient world. The politician, the thinker, the man of religion, the man in the street, and supremely the Jew, all alike were looking for 'salvation'.[3]

Simeon and Anna are representative of this Jewish expectation.

GOD'S 'PREPARATIONS'

The preparations of God go back a very long way, far longer and deeper than any human expectations. And necessarily so, for His preparations were to encompass the salvation of the world: 'My eyes have seen your salvation, which you have prepared in the sight of all people' (Luke 2:30–31), as well as the cosmos itself. His work of preparation began with the making known of His covenant purposes to Abraham, with whom He promised to flood the world with the light of His blessings. It continued through the stunning glimpses of His glory, which He gives in and through one particular nation, Israel. It went on throughout the centuries by the sending of Spirit-inspired prophets, messengers whom He entrusted with His vision statement for the salvation of the world.

Inspired with the self-same Spirit, Simeon sings a prophetic précis of what he saw of God's future. With great joy Simeon feels himself to be gloriously alive in the moment when his expectations and God's preparations meet in a deeply satisfying way. It is to Simeon, then, that we owe this superb summary of God's unique 'vision statement' (Luke 2:30–32).

At this point Simeon turns to the child's mother and begins to speak prophetically about his future:

> This child is destined for the falling and rising of many in Israel, and to be a sign that will be opposed so that the inner thoughts of many will be revealed – and a sword will pierce your own soul too.
>
> Luke 2:34–35, NRSV

Here is the divine *mission statement*, matching as it does the divine vision statement of verses 30–32. And the mission statement of God defines the mission of Jesus.

But now a shadow is cast over the Song, over the blessing and over the wondering hearts of the parents. It's as if the long shadow of the cross falls across Simeon's satisfied face, darkening those peaceful eyes. When God's long-prepared salvation arrives, it is not to everyone's liking. For when God's prepared salvation and people's presumed expectations meet, they don't so much converge as collide. This mission of Jesus – to make real His Father's vision of salvation – causes unwelcome consternation, provokes upheaval, arouses opposition, exposes self-serving agendas and self-centred motives. All of which needs spelling out in more detail.

THE UPHEAVAL HE CAUSES

The mission of Jesus will cause the most massive, internal upheaval in the life of His nation, bringing about 'the falling and rising of many in Israel'. His coming will effect what amounts to a dying of the old Israel and the resurrection of a renewed Israel. This is a revolution that is not accidental but one that is quite deliberately in the plan of God. Jesus is 'set' or 'destined' to have this effect, not unlike Isaiah's 'stone of stumbling' (Isa. 8:14; 28:16; cf. Luke 20:17,18).

THE OPPOSITION HE AROUSES

As a sign pointing to God's long-prepared salvation, Simeon said that Jesus would be 'a sign that will be spoken against' (Luke 2:34b), facing fierce, embittered opposition from those who thought they knew better. And Jesus certainly did face this. Scribes, lawyers, Torah experts all interrogated and criticised Him. They looked for cunning ways to entrap and accuse Him and were not unwilling to participate in His execution. His home town synagogue in Nazareth, God's home town, was the scene of His first big rejection. Jerusalem was the scene of His final rejection. It was opposition – all the way to Golgotha.

THE SECRETS HE REVEALS

Jesus would prove to be a blinding spotlight 'so that the thoughts of many will be revealed'. He would expose the hidden agendas, the twisted logic, the malicious motives and the jealous and self-serving attitudes behind the religious masks of the nation's leaders (cf. Luke 5:21,22; 6:8; 12:16–21; 20:9–18). He publicly stripped the disguise away, unforgivably unmasking them. No wonder they came to hate His presence. How gently He comforted the disturbed; how rudely He disturbed the comfortable.

THE PAIN HE CAUSES

Jesus' mission would bring unavoidable pain to His nearest and dearest, as His mother was warned: 'and a sword shall pierce your own soul too'. Her lot was one of misunderstanding, bewilderment and early bereavement – thereby nobly representing Israel as the sword went through the heart of the nation's life (cf. Ezek. 14:17). A people long prepared by their prophets for God's salvation, for the long-awaited deliverance from oppression, is now itself needing to repent (Luke 1:16,76–79; 3:13,14).

Faced with the challenge of Jesus' mission, Israel itself was deeply divided.

Nonetheless, this was Jesus' destiny, the harsh reality of His mission. Not everyone was to like Him; not everyone welcomed, blessed or thanked God for Him, as Simeon and Anna did. Indeed, some cursed Him and God because of Him. Not everyone saw in Him the salvation of the world and glory for Israel. Since light for the world meant glory for Israel, this was resented by some; and because glory for Israel meant light for the world, this was equally resented by others. So he was opposed and contradicted by sinners (Heb. 12:3). Yet both reactions – rejection and acceptance – were inevitable, because His coming brought both judgment and grace.

God's vision is salvation: a light to the Gentiles and glory for Israel. Jesus' mission is to put flesh on the vision, whatever it cost Him in pain, provocation or persecution. Are we, as the Church, willing to pay the price of God's vision? The vision statements of today may deceive us by covering up the harsh realities of the mission statements. But not here! For here God's vision and Jesus' mission merge as one. Today's vision statements may be airy-fairy PR fantasies: easy to conjure up and more enjoyable than actually doing the real work of achieving set goals. Well, not here. So while the Church seeks to clarify its vision, let it not forget its mission and let it be prepared to pay the price of the vision by getting on with the mission.

ANNA AND GOD'S MISSION

The prophetess Anna represents exactly God's mission. She models a prophetic understanding of God's Messiah as the key to the saving purposes of God in history. This is a seriously devout and righteous woman, prayerful and faithful in her devotion to Yahweh and the faith of Israel: 'She never left the temple but worshipped night and day, fasting and praying' (Luke 2:37). Anna is numbered among those who, like Simeon, and Joseph of Arimathea (Luke 23:50,51), are waiting for the coming of the kingdom of God that will bring consolation to Israel and redemption to Jerusalem.

The response of this beautiful old lady (whether she was eighty-four years of age or had been a widow for that length of time is unclear from the original text) is wonderful and instructive. Her immediate and quite instinctive reaction to her dramatic encounter with the Hope of all her years is to worship – 'she gave thanks to God' – and to witness – 'and she spoke about the child to all who were looking forward to the redemption of Jerusalem'. About this incident, John Nolland keenly observes: 'The dignity of old age, a deep passion for God, and prophetic inspiration, stand behind and give credibility to, her witness to Jesus.'[4] Giving thanks to God for Jesus and telling the world about Him – this lies at the heart of what Luke the evangelist sees as the mission of a Spirit-inspired Church.

CHAPTER FOURTEEN

His Majesty the Baby

Read Matthew 2:1–23

> The first thing a baby does when he comes into the world is to establish his kingdom. He, of course, is the king. He is number one. Because there is none higher than himself, he is in the position of a god. Shortly after birth, the baby is hungry. He is exhausted by a humiliating eviction from quarters which, quite frankly, he thoroughly enjoyed. Besides, his source of food is cut off. A complaint must be registered immediately. The baby cries. He wants service. His food arrives, his nappies are changed … Each time the king cries out, he is obeyed. All he has to do is cry and someone will come running to attend to his needs. Obviously, he is the centre of the world. The world exists for him. He is a god![1]

Here is, as Freud termed him, 'his majesty the baby'. Tragically some people never outgrow this stage; Herod was one of them. Herod fell prey to that perennial babyhood that afflicts men of power: that obsessive self-centredness that brooks no dissent and inflicts such untold suffering on others. Herod 'the Great' he was called, but in fact he was a ruthless, tyrannical ego-maniac who killed half his family to secure his rule.

Part Jewish, part Idumean, he became governor of Galilee in 47 BC. A decade of fluctuating fortunes and much barbarity later, Herod was installed – with backing from the Romans – as king of the Jews in 37 BC. His regime was threatened by the turbulence within the Roman Empire, especially that surrounding

Antony and Cleopatra. But with Antony's defeat and death at the battle of Actium in 31 BC, Herod managed to persuade the victorious Octavius of his loyalty to Rome – and Octavius confirmed his royal status. This was soon sealed by Herod's gift to Octavius of 800 talents.

Kept in power by the Roman legions, Herod consolidated his reign by executing forty-five of the wealthiest citizens, confiscating their properties. He engaged in extensive building programmes, filling the country with temples and monuments dedicated to Caesar. He lavished gifts on the emperor and other imperial figures, becoming patron of a number of Greek cities and sponsoring the Olympic Games.

For his own family he built magnificent palaces in Jerusalem as well as impressive fortresses at Herodian and Masada. His pet project – perhaps imagining himself as some latter-day Solomon – was the rebuilding of the Temple in Jerusalem. The system of taxation he imposed to pay for all these schemes and projects was extremely oppressive and much resented. Herod was, according to Richard Horsley, 'bleeding his country and people to death'.[2] Here truly was 'his majesty the baby', entirely at the mercy of his all-demanding ego.

Not surprisingly, with more to lose than most, Herod is alarmed when some strange Eastern men arrived to enquire: 'Where is the child who has been born king of the Jews? For we … have come to pay him homage' (Matt. 2:2, NRSV). 'King of the Jews?' Herod could well have replied, 'but they have one already, don't they?' It is hard for us to realise just how politically explosive Jesus was. The alarm of Herod and the Jerusalem authorities is the first sign of the immense political impact Jesus would make. The same note is struck throughout the infancy narratives (see Luke 1:46–53; 2:34).

ENORMOUS POLITICAL WAVES

Jesus was not born into a Christmas-card fantasy world: an idyllic, romanticised haven of sentimentality and peace. The world He was born into was racked with economic oppression and political turbulence, and His coming made enormous political waves. Ben Witherington helpfully spells this out:

> The image of a gentle Jesus meek and mild going about Galilee offering entertaining stories called parables or engaging in abstract academic debates about various religious notions fails to convey the sensitive and sometimes hostile atmosphere in which Jesus operated and the effect his teaching would have had on those who lived in this environment. It was an atmosphere in which politics and religion were almost always mixed, and Messianic claims, actions or ideas were normally viewed by those in power as threats to the political status quo.[3]

There can be no doubting that Herod saw it like this. For suddenly he found himself embroiled with his chief advisors in intense discussion about who the real king and messiah of Israel was and where he was to be found. His blood pressure would have risen sharply at any implication that he didn't fit the bill: 'Why are we talking about anyone else? And in any case why take this supposed messiah so seriously?'

We know that there were several would-be messianic claimants in and around the time of Jesus; so what is so threatening about this one? After all, 'messiahs' come and go all the time without causing this much trouble (see Matt. 24:23,24). Some go to their ignominious death; others can't take the pressure and quit. Perhaps Herod and his advisors sensed that the real Messiah had arrived and would neither buckle under pressure nor quit! The Bible scholars are consulted (Matt. 2:4–6). Their answer to the question 'where' is Bethlehem – if they care to believe the prophet Micah (Micah 5:2). Two intriguing points immediately arise here: first, they knew the proof texts but, as has been said, they 'didn't lift a sandal' to do anything about it. Such is the inertia of academic passivity. Second, the star was not enough without the Scriptures. The followers of the star were led to the light of the Scriptures.

Maybe, like the Magi, you've travelled long and far in search of truth and reality, love and justice. Complete your journey by coming to Jesus. He is where your star stops; He is the end of the search and the beginning of the quest. Bow to Him as Lord and King, rise with faith and overwhelming satisfaction that a lifelong thirst is quenched and a lifetime's dream fulfilled.

The ensuing joy is graphically told by Tolkein in his own inimitable way as Sam asks Gandalf what's happened to the world? 'A great shadow has departed', said Gandalf. 'I feel like spring after winter, and sun on the leaves, and like trumpets and harps and all the songs I have ever heard.'[4]

G.K. Chesterton evokes the same mood but in quieter vein:

> To an open house at evening
> Home shall men come
> To an older town than Eden
> To a taller town than Rome
> To the end of the way of the wandering star
> To the things that cannot be and that are
> To the place where God was homeless
> And all men are at home.[5]

The summary by Matthew the evangelist is terse by contrast, yet captures the excitement to the point of spilling over into tautology: 'They rejoiced with exceeding great joy!' (Matt. 2:10, AV). Then they offered gifts, bowed down and worshipped the 'Immanuel', this unique, God-with-us child. Again the contrast is sharp between the desire of the Gentile astrologers to acknowledge the Messiah and the apathy of the Jewish leaders who did not, apparently, even take the trouble to go to Bethlehem!

FULFILMENT IN JESUS

Matthew saw – and he wants his readers to see – what the Jerusalem Bible-experts didn't. If the wise men seeking satisfaction in their search for truth find it in Jesus, so the prophetic hopes raised by the first Exodus of a greater and ultimate liberation by God are likewise finding their fulfilment in Jesus. By 'fulfilled' we remind ourselves that Matthew means us to understand that the long story of Israel has reached its climax in Jesus Himself. Jesus is to be seen as the crucial chapter in the story of God's salvation. As Donald A. Hagner comments: 'Jesus relives, sums up, brings to fruition, all the history and experience of his people.'[6] All the promises, prophecies, patterns and passion of Israel are gathered up and brought to the moment of realisation in Jesus.

The king in danger becomes a refugee! What a familiar scenario this was in the twentieth-century: whispers in the night, frantic packing, handcarts overloaded with whatever can be salvaged, family treasures clutched fiercely by anxious refugees from tyranny, trudging along country roads in search of safety. This is 'God-with-us', sharing our human condition to the full; entering into His people's 'exile' all over again. So, as a result of Joseph's dream, Jesus goes down into Egypt as the Israelites were once brought to Egypt by Joseph's dream at the beginning of their story.

The theological point here is an important one. God's self-revelation has three facets. The first is: He reveals Himself in *creation*, in the natural world, in sun and moon and stars. Theologians call this 'general revelation'. The second is: He reveals Himself in *the Bible*, in the scriptural record of His dealings with the patriarchs and the people of Israel. This is usually termed 'special revelation'. The third is: He reveals Himself in *Jesus*, this is known as 'saving revelation'.

The point here is clear: the light of the star must lead us to the light of the Scriptures for a true understanding of Who God is. Yet above and beyond this, the star and the Scriptures will point us to Jesus, the true Light of the world, the saving revelation in Whom God supremely reveals Himself. In Frederick Dale Bruner's neat summary:

> God's revelation in nature raises the question and begins the quest; God's revelation in Scriptures gives the answer and directs the quest to the goal; God's revelation in Christ-the-goal satisfies the quest.[7]

What then are we to make of the Magi (Matt. 2:7–12)? Bruner again:

> The invitation of the Magi to the coming-out party of Christ indicates the deep and wide mercy of God that Matthew had either found or inserted in his Old Testament genealogical studies.[8]

The Wise Men seeking satisfaction in their search for truth found it in Jesus. And wise men still do! These astrologers from Persia or Babylon, as probably they were, have reached their goal guided by a comet or an unusual conjunction of the planets in what was the original star trek. By following a star they arrived at the Light. Familiar with Jewish expectations of deliverance from their own study and contact with Jewish communities in the East, these men are alerted by the star-sign to the imminent fulfilment of their hopes and dreams. Willing to submit themselves to Israel's prophetic Scriptures, they hurry, in response, to Bethlehem.

A NEW EXODUS

As we have seen, what Matthew is therefore doing at this point, in evoking Hosea's recollection of the Exodus, is to paint a picture of *a new Exodus in Jesus, Who embodies Israel's vocation and destiny*. If the Wise Men sensed even a fraction of this, then they failed to enlighten Herod who, enraged even more, ordered a cull of every child under two years of age in the Bethlehem area (Matt. 2:16). What follows is the terrible 'massacre of the innocents'. Popular imagination usually thinks in terms of many hundreds. But analysts reckon that at the time Bethlehem had no more than a thousand inhabitants, with some sixty births taking place in any two-year period. If half were boys and half of these survived infancy, then probably only about eighteen children were slaughtered. But to say 'only' is a travesty of truth. That still leaves three dozen brokenhearted parents, a profound and unbearable tragedy.

The ghastly paradox of the first Christmas remains: the birth of Jesus led to the death of these children; the joy of His coming was overshadowed by the bereavement of so many inhabitants of Bethlehem. The 'massacre of the innocents' is the immediate, deadly price paid for His coming. If they had known of Herod's draconian logic, many mothers in Bethlehem would have wished that Jesus had never been born.

Could Jesus' birth have seen less bloody consequences? Perhaps; but this is the way our world is. The Bethlehem massacre opens up the wider question: Why do the innocent suffer in our world? There are no answers here, let alone easy ones. But some considerations are worth offering. Historically, a failure to acknowledge the sovereignty of God in the form of this one child does lead to unimaginable cruelty to children. Remove all restraints in society, give free reign to rampant egos and to the perennial babyhood of self-willed adults, and eventually it's those at the bottom of the pile who suffer most: battered wives and abused children. So: Why do the innocent suffer? Why did God allow *these* innocent to suffer death? Frankly, there is no answer. Yet at least we now know, with incarnational certainty, that God is not immune from the injustice and pain of the world He created and chooses to sustain. In Jesus Christ we trace the narratives of a God Who makes Himself vulnerable to human pain, sin and suffering. This God embraces risk in sharing the human condition, in facing the danger and feeling the fear. And before long, this 'Immanuel', this innocent of all innocents, will die, the 'just for the unjust'.

HE HAS COME FOR ALL OF US

He has come for us who, like the Magi, are 'aliens', foreigners to the covenants of promise, without God and, apart from Him, without hope in the world. He has come for us who, like Herod, are rebels on the inside, refusing to bow before Christ's Lordship and majesty. He has come for all the innocent victims and grieving parents, for all who are not only sinners but sufferers and victims too. For them this Messiah has come to save from sins and to be God-with-them. He will not quit under pressure; He is the genuine article. God's saving purpose, begun with Abraham, will not be thwarted by bondage in Egypt, by the failure of kings, by the tragedy of Exile, and certainly not now by the hatred of puppet rulers like Herod – nor by the soon-coming crisis of crucifixion.

By quoting from the prophet Jeremiah, as we have noted before, Matthew is recalling the trauma of the Babylonian Exile six centuries earlier. Just as Rachel – the original mother of Israel – was to be lamenting the fate of her descendants exiled to Babylon, so now, Matthew suggests, she weeps again, this time in sympathy with the mothers of Bethlehem at a further crisis point in the history of her people. Matthew is very subtly and skillfully probing the texture of Scripture here. Already he has noted that the demise of the Davidic kingship at the Exile is a key to his presentation of the significance of Jesus (Matt. 1:11,17). Now it is being made clear, in Don Carson's words, that

> the tears associated with exile will end ... the tears known in Jeremiah's day are climaxed and ended by the tears of the mothers of Bethlehem. The heir to David's throne has come, the exile is over, the true Son of God has arrived, and he will introduce the new covenant promised by Jeremiah.[9]

For this, God's time has come and God's child has come! 'Where is he who is has been born king of the Jews?' is a question that, in the end, finds its answer not on a brass nameplate on his crib but on the crude logo written above his head on the cross.

SHARP CONTRAST

Herod's response to the infant Christ seems to stand as an intentionally sharp contrast with that of the Magi. Indeed his reaction to the newborn baby epitomises and foreshadows the official reaction to the mature man. But the hopes and dreams of both Jews and Gentiles find their satisfaction here. The Magi sense this, where Israel's official representatives do not. These Magi come, and see, and are conquered – and go home rejoicing. This one *is* 'His majesty the baby'; He is the still centre of the world. This baby *is* God! He has only to come to be worshipped; He has only to cry to be obeyed.

CHAPTER FIFTEEN

Ready-Made or Self-Assembly?

Read Luke 2:39–40, 52; 19:45–20:8

And the central character of these nativity stories? What became of Him? What happened next?

It is a unique characteristic of our humanness that we do not enter the world ready-made but require to be, so to speak, self-assembled. Since we are not the finished article from 'day one', there lies before us the lifelong task of becoming fully human. And most of us believe the task to be worth the effort, with only a few sad souls giving up prematurely and entirely. To be truly, fully human is a noble ambition and a great vocation. This was the vocation that Jesus accepted, the journey He embarked upon.

So it was that Jesus 'went down to Nazareth with them and was obedient to them' (Luke 2:51). His full submission to the law was matched by His full submission to the requirements of the human family. It was here, in the hidden years, that He learnt the obedience that was to be the path to His maturity in later years. So with us, as Oswald Chambers observed: 'When we are born from above and the Son of God is formed in us, it is not the passing of the years that matures his life in us but our obedience.'[1]

PROGRESS REPORTS

Luke provides us with two early progress reports (Luke 2:40,52), noting steady development by Jesus on all fronts. If combined they read: 'The child grew and became strong, filled with wisdom, and the favour of

God was upon him, as well as the goodwill of men.' He grew physically 'strong ... in stature'. No cardboard cut-out figure emerges here but a real man with real feelings, with expendable energy levels like the rest of us, with a physique honed in the manual, workday world of a carpentry business. He also grew mentally and 'was filled with wisdom'. Not for Him the problem of information overload we suffer with today. Instead, Jesus was able to develop a unique sensitivity to the Creator's world out of which true insight is born.

He also grew spiritually 'in favour with God', developing His trust, faith and discernment through prayer and the reading of the Hebrew Scriptures. Austin Farrer has noted:

> He was not a copy-book man in general. He was a Galilean carpenter, a freelance rabbi; and he wove his life, as each of us must, out of the raw materials that were to hand. He found his way by groping and he knew his Father by trusting. Only he made no false moves.[2]

Jesus also grew socially, 'in favour with men'. He was well able to relate to relatives and friends, clients and customers. He grew to be Someone Who would attract strong men to Him, be at ease with women and be a magnet for children. This 'fine and fair' man did not come ready-made. It was life with Mary and Joseph, with friends, schoolmates, relatives and customers that shaped His human and divine life.

Luke finally notes that 'the grace of God was upon him' (Luke 2:40) so that He grew up with a balanced sense of self-esteem, secure in the love of His heavenly

Father, knowing the freedom and favour of God, even as He submitted and obeyed.

THE FAMILY ALBUM

Did Luke sit down to tea with Mary one cool summer evening and ask to see the family snapshot album? Did they peruse together the photos of her eldest and dearest?

> Look at this one ... a toddler covered in wood shavings! Now this one ... My! How quickly he grew up ... quite a sturdy boy there ... he was always shinning up that sycamore tree into his tree house. And not afraid of hard work later ... humping some wood into the yard by the look of it ... bit impetuous when he was small though ... this is him with his hand bandaged – got hold of the wrong end of his father's chisel as I recall ... Now there he is down at Galilee with his father fishing. And that's his pet rabbit and his wild flower collection ... he was always fascinated with things around him. 'Wise head on young shoulders', Elizabeth said ... That's us, off to the synagogue ... and that's me reading the old Israel stories to him ... he liked me doing that ... Oh yes, I took that one without him knowing – he used to pray a lot by that stream ...
>
> Socially? Well, he had a lot of friends ... it's here somewhere ... yes, here it is: a birthday party with his mates ... laughing their heads off at some joke, by the look of it... and this one, I remember it well: the lads and the girls of the village playing weddings and funerals ... he played the flute but not very well.

> Did he get on well with people? Well, yes, he did ... everyone seemed to take a liking to him ... the customers liked him ... There he is with Joseph, shaking hands with farmer Elias ... They'd just delivered the yoke he ordered, you see ... But did I ever tell you about the time when he was twelve – just coming up to his Bar-Mitzvah? Now that was a strange business ... we couldn't figure it out for years ... All I can say is that it seemed really, really important ... so I just stored it away in my heart ... Anyhow, Luke, you can tell that particular story.

LUKE'S STORY

The way Luke recounts the event seems like the classic parental nightmare. The twelve-year-old has gone AWOL. The crowds are thick at the festival and He's slipped off somewhere. The parents feel awful; they'd assumed He was with other members of the pilgrimage, that some family members were looking after Him. Even worse, they hadn't noticed He was missing for the best part of the day. Now they are frantically searching for Him everywhere with that high-octane mixture of alarm and anger that Luke himself understates as 'acute anxiety' (see Luke 2:48). Their anxiety gives way to sheer 'astonishment' when they eventually find Him, because they discover their young son in the Temple precincts debating theology with the elite, professional Torah-teachers (Luke 2:46,47). Jesus was lost in lively discussion with the experts, an 'eager-beaver' of a student, inquisitive, curious and learning fast on the job. So much so that some of His answers and insights delighted and amazed everyone.

Then followed a scene dreaded by every twelve-year-old: His parents turn up to embarrass Him by their desperation, anxiety and anger. What they have to say to Him is classic parent-speak. The scolding words come pouring out: 'We've been worried sick ... out of our minds. Why have you treated us like this? ... It was our special treat to let you come up to the festival this year – a year before time ... now look how you've repaid us ... after all we've done for you too ... we thought we could trust you ...' All in all, a predictable script!

ENTIRELY BAFFLING

What Jesus says to them is altogether unexpected: strange, mysterious and baffling. 'Why were you searching for me? Didn't you know I had to be in my Father's house?' But they for their part 'did not understand what he was saying to them' (Luke 2:50). Not the first time parents bemoan the fact that they don't understand their children. As one girl said: 'My mother and I have a perfect understanding: I don't understand her and she doesn't understand me!'

But what is it about their son they don't understand? Surely they remember Gabriel's stunning annunciation and the old priest Simeon with his startling prophecy? So why are they uncomprehending? Is it because at this precise moment a larger world than their own small parochial one suddenly opens up to them? Is it that Jesus is hinting at being part of a much bigger story than that of their familiar family one; that domestic concerns would be better subsumed into caring passionately about the things of God? Is it that most of our fears – about what to eat, drink, wear – could be resolved if we sought first God's kingdom and His righteousness?

Remarkably, significantly, movingly and tellingly, Luke explains how the boy Jesus returned to Nazareth with His parents and became obedient to them (Luke 2:51). From then on and for ever more He became known as 'Jesus of Nazareth'. He took His developing humanness and sowed it back into the soil of obedient and respectful submission to His parents in this particular town. He immersed Himself in the developing task of becoming human.

BECOMING HUMAN

One of my favourite authors, Daniel Taylor, has written a book called *Letters to My Children*. Here's a sample.

> Papa: what were you like when you were a kid?
> Dear Children: smart, cute, lovable, talented, kind and humble! – next question!
> Papa: what about sex?
> Dear Children: I'm too busy: ask your mother: love Papa!
> Papa: what should we be when we grow up?
> Dear Children: Don't spend too much time worrying about what you are going to be. Think about what you are.
> Because what you are going to be is being

> decided right now.
> You are making choices. And the decisions you make will matter, today, tomorrow, and for ever.
> I love you guys and I pray that God will help you to choose wisely.
> Love Papa.[3]

'What shall I become when I grow up?' Did Jesus ever ask that question of Joseph and Mary? If so, I wonder how they responded to it? Did they:

- tell Him: 'This is what you are: a child of the covenant'?
- tell Him the Old Testament story of His people and His God?
- teach Him to pray, to trust and to learn well from the old scrolls?

Where did He learn this? In what school?

When a member of Tony Blair's first New Labour cabinet sent her son, not to the state schools that her party had championed before the election but to a fee-paying school with a better educational reputation, she was, not surprisingly, accused of hypocrisy.

'Hypocrisy' is the feigning of virtues or beliefs or standards: actions inconsistent with one's stated aims or policy. The term derives from the Greek word *hypocrites* used of an actor wearing a mask on stage!

Now, if you'd been God, what school would you have sent your Son to?

Divine policy, remember, as outlined in the manifesto,

is to give itself fully in order to restore human life to its redeemed potential and destiny. Perhaps a *Roman* school would suit? There He would have learned law, military affairs, engineering. Or a *Greek* school? There He could have studied philosophy, rhetoric, logic, medicine, art. Maybe a place could be found at a *Greek drama* school. There He could learn to be a *hypocrite* – to masquerade as a man; to be a god disguised as a man but not really human; in short, to play the human role without really being one.

But God in His infinite wisdom sent Him to a *Jewish* school in Israel. In this school there was only one textbook – the Hebrew Scriptures, which He studied from early childhood (1 Tim. 3:16). From this He would have learned that Israel had been intended to be the embodiment of a new kind of humanity for the sake of the world. He would have learned about the goodness of creation affirming, unlike some Greeks, the high value of human physicality. He would have learned that Israel was the testing ground for a new Adamic race, a people redeemed and recalled to live in covenant faithfulness with God.

He would have learned that pain and suffering were an integral part of His people's story. He would have discovered in His own way that Israel, in Arthur Koestler's words, was the 'exposed nerve of the human race'. He would have learned, as He would *not* have done in a Roman school, to pursue the power of love rather than the love of power. He would have learned the Scriptures that make you wise to a salvation that lies on the other side of exile and return, death and resurrection. In short, He would have studied the humanities and graduated in the 'university of life'.

SECOND TIME AROUND

Twenty years after His boyhood drama, Jesus took His mature manhood back to the Temple in Jerusalem. Once again He held court there, the people once more spellbound by His teaching (Luke 19:45–20:8). Once again He engaged the professional theologians in debate. But this time He caused a massive disruption of the Temple's routine. He staged a dramatic, prophetic demonstration, which said in effect that Jerusalem was not large enough to contain both Him and the Temple. One would have to go. This time He is interrogated fiercely: 'By what authority are you saying and doing these things?' 'Is it lawful to pay taxes to Caesar?' Question piled on question. Again, as twenty-one years earlier, He astounds them with His answers. This time they understand only too clearly the threat this young Nazarene poses to their vested self-interest … and they relapse into bitter, hate-filled silence (Luke 20:26).

WHAT AN EXCEPTION

Mary and Joseph didn't understand why Jesus went back to the Temple the first time. And it's difficult for us to understand fully why He went there for the last time, except only that it was to do with His zeal for His Father's house, His consuming concern for His

Father's affairs, His passionate conviction that our humanness was worth saving. The great Temple in Jerusalem, the very dwelling place on earth of the One, True, Creator God, which He had first visited as a twelve-year-old, He now gazed up at as a thirty-three-year-old mature man. And gazing at it, He predicted its downfall. 'Not one stone will be left standing', He declared, anticipating the terrible crisis that befell the city of God and the sanctuary, forty years on at the hands of the armies of imperial Rome. Yet before its stones would be torn down, He Himself would be 'torn apart' on a cross, His humanness 'dismembered' piece by piece. Then, in the mighty act of resurrection, His Father would put His humanness together again and, with Him, raise up a new Temple, not made with hands, one that would be the true house of His Father.

Gathering up the reflections of this chapter, we need to underline that *our humanness is a God-given vocation*. Also that *our humanness is worth working at each day*. And our progress to full humanness is the *one, great adventure we are all offered*. Further, that in order to reclaim true humanness for us it was worth God's Son *becoming one of us, then growing, then dying, as one of us*. And we recall that Jesus was *never a self-made man; He was a God-made man*. And so must we be if we are to become fully human. This entails allowing Him in His love to take us to pieces and gradually remake us by His death and resurrection.

One day the result may be that we turn out to be remarkably like Him.

CHAPTER SIXTEEN

The Journey

(Re-)Read Matthew 1–2; Luke 2:1–2

As we draw to a close these reflections on the birth and nativity of Jesus what, I wonder, has been our personal journey in the reading of this book. How far have we come as readers and listeners, and where will we go from here? Let's remind ourselves now of the distance travelled by the original characters in the story

MARY AND JOSEPH

A fifteen-year-old girl and an eighteen-year-old youth from a local carpentry business – betrothed as they are in binding compact but not yet married – set out on a ninety-mile journey from Nazareth southwards to Bethlehem, a four- or five-day trip. The girl is heavily pregnant and for the past nine months has been holding in her heart an incredible secret: 'Do not be afraid … you have found favour with God … you will conceive by the Holy Spirit and bear a son … name him Jesus …. Davidic king … Son of God …'. The young man, still bemused by all this but encouraged by a dream to go along with it, is no doubt nursing his anxiety about how she will cope with the journey.

They arrive to find Bethlehem hopelessly crowded. They seek lodging with relatives but with no space available in the main area of the house, they bed down in the caravanserai at the back. There, sharing space with the animals, she gives birth to her son and lays Him in a feeding trough. If we ask what brought them from Nazareth to Bethlehem, the answer is simple:

taxation. The summons came at an economically difficult time when ordinary people suffered under an oppressive taxation system. It is understood that there were three layers of tax: tithes to their Jerusalem priesthood; taxes to Herod, their extravagant, ruthless puppet king; and tribute to their colonial masters at Rome. So here the summons goes out in Caesar Augustus' name. The irony is underplayed by Luke the evangelist. Caesar plays his imperial card, lays his tax demand on the table, and unwittingly plays straight into the hands of the sovereign God!

Ordinary people with eyes to see trace a thread woven by God into the texture of all our human stories. Even circumstances outside our control, things we would never choose to happen to us and would prefer not to happen to us, even the dictat and summons of an unjust imperial power, even things we surely resent, God can use to bring about His purpose and bring us to the turning-point of our lives. There we discover that the very reason for being alive is *to be in a close personal relationship with Jesus*. Was it *this* defining truth that dawned on Mary and Joseph as they gazed down on His tiny face? Was this the moment when they sensed that it had all been worthwhile – the moment of journey's end and journey's beginning?

THE SHEPHERDS

These ordinary working men are herdsmen on the night shift, idling away the long hours with the usual small talk and wisecracks, banter and gentle argument, mulling over the local chariot-racing results and how good breakfast will be. Suddenly, our rural peasants are bathed in a strange and eerie radiance, as if the glory of God had spilled over from heaven to earth. An angelic messenger appears, scaring the daylight into them! He delivers personal good news and personal directions to go and look for a child born in a cattle-trough, a child Who is Israel's Messiah, the world's Saviour, the *Lord* Himself! As if this is not enough, the air is filled with the stunning singing of unearthly voices and words the like of which have never been heard before: 'Glory to God … peace on earth …'

Unearthly as this extraordinary event was, it was also politically red-hot, even revolutionary, in its implications. Wasn't Rome's peace, the famed *Pax Romana*, the guarantee of the world's stability? Hadn't Caesar Augustus just proclaimed himself saviour? In the face of Roman propaganda, which declared Augustus divine saviour and overlord, could this infant be the answer to those unnumbered cries of the world's oppressed and poor for freedom and justice?

As the strange light dimmed and the ethereal voices faded on the night air, these shepherds deserve credit for not just slumping to the ground, moonstruck. Up they get and off they go, like mad things, hoofing it down the hill and around the lodging houses of Bethlehem until they find what they've been told to look for. Bursting in, they blurt out their extraordinary story to Mary and Joseph, then head off back to their work, praising and glorifying God for all they had seen and heard! They return to a familiar working life that would, however, never be the same again; for they had lost their shepherds' hearts to God's choicest lamb!

And if we were to ask: What got them to take off the way they did, swooping down to sleeping Bethlehem? The answer is *a sudden interruption of their routine*, a shock that disrupted their normal patterns, a stupendous surprise, a moment of dazzling revelation that awoke them to another world. It was supernatural, it was scary, it was stunning. Briefly and unforgettably, it lifted them above the mundane realm of making ends meet, of moaning about the weather or the government. And they didn't stay there transfixed, sucking their religious thumbs or twittering on about their paranormal experience. Rather, 'not disobedient to the heavenly vision' they came, saw and were conquered by Christ. They believed and got happy.

THE MAGI

What exactly was it that motivated the Magi to make their arduous journey to Bethlehem? It's understood that these were neither kings nor necessarily three in number (tradition assumed that the three gifts of gold, incense and myrrh were presented by three persons, whereas the Scriptures certainly make no mention of three individuals). In all likelihood they were priestly astrologers from one of the Eastern kingdoms that had been overrun by Rome's all-conquer-ing armies. From proud nations resentful of Roman domination – something the Magi had in common with the Jews – these 'Wise Men' came on the look-out for signs and portents of a new age, an age of liberation from the yoke of Roman totalitarian oppression. Theirs, then, was not only a political quest, but also an intellectual one born of curiosity. So if we ask what brought them on their journey, the answer is: *a search for truth and justice.*

Their star-assisted search was one for the world's Deliverer; and in pursuit of Him they arrive at Herod's court to alarm this corrupt king with their talk of a 'king of the Jews'. And what they discover is that true wisdom is not found in the East, the route so many continue to take in our day. Nor, for that matter, is it found in the West with its materialism, intellectual scepticism and post-Enlightenment loss of meaning. True wisdom is found only in Jesus. Life's meaning is not written in the stars after all, as if astrology and horoscopes can crack the code. But all the signs and all the stars point to Jesus. In Him alone is our true and eternal destiny spelled out for us. The gifts brought by the Magi speak volumes: gold for a king, frankincense for priesthood and, mysteriously and ominously, myrrh for embalming the dead, in itself an odd gift for a baby. Frederick Buechner memorably comments:

> I tell you two terrible things. What we saw on the face of the new-born child was his death … it sat on his head like a crown, this death he would die. And we saw, as sure as the earth beneath our feet, that to stay with him would be to share that death. And now, my brothers, I ask you

a terrible question and God knows I ask it also of myself. Is the truth beyond all truths, beyond the stars, just this: *that to live without him is the real death, that to die with him is the only life?*[1]

THE CHILD

How far had He travelled? Certainly a nine-month, intrauterine journey from conception to the light of day. But the answer the first Christians gave was to the effect that He had come on a much longer journey than anyone yet born. Before the foundation of the earth, beyond the limits of the natural world He *was*: 'In the beginning was the Word, and the Word was with God, and the Word was God ... the Word became a human being and lived among us'. This is the measure of how far He had journeyed. Out of the infinite distance He had come, into the finite nearness; out of the warm heart of the eternal nature of God to the cold shoulder of an indifferent world. In the peculiar language He Himself was to later use, He came as a result of a 'sending'. 'I was sent ...' was to be Jesus' characteristic way of putting it, sent by the divine Sender as a divine gift; sent on a divine mission – 'You shall call his name Jesus for he shall *save his people from their sins*'.

And in case we get 'hung up' on 'coming down' language, we venture another way of putting it by saying: He had come from much nearer than we might imagine. For God is all around us – 'in him we live and move and have our being'. He is closer to us than hands and feet, nearer than breathing or the beat of our hearts. Suddenly, and scarily, this God gets even closer, more seeable and touchable than ever before; taking shape and form in one particular place, in one particular face and set of fingers. And this child is 'Immanuel: God-with-us'.

In this human appearing, the truly human One, the one Creator God, has got inside human skin, inside our humanity, feeling our feelings, fighting our battles, facing our pressures and, before He's middle-aged, dying our death for us. And if now we let Him in, living our life for us.

The Old Testament story of this God should have prepared us for all this. From the beginning He shows Himself to be a God Who longs for close-up fellowship with His human creatures. The book of Genesis has the daring view of Him taking a stroll with Adam and Eve in the cool of the day. This sets the tone for the glimpses we get of Him as a God journeying across the wilderness with His people, pledging to be with them every step of the way; reassuringly present as a pillar of cloud by day and a pillar of fire by night, visible signs of His presence with His people. This mobile God is worshipped in a portable sanctuary or tabernacle where He could be met right at the centre of His people's ongoing life. He adapts Himself to the rhythms of making and breaking camp. He stays with them as they journey to their promised land.

Matthew's genealogy, as we saw, recalled this. From Abraham to David the quest was to find and establish a home for God's people, Israel, in the land. The phase from David to the Exile was concerned with building and maintaining (and in the end losing) a home for God in the midst of His people: the Temple in Jerusalem, His dwelling place on earth. From the Exile onwards began again the task of finding a domicile for both Israel and Israel's God where, once again, they could dwell together. *Now, in Jesus, both sinners and exiles can come home to dwell with God as He comes to make His home with them.* To look at Jesus is truly to see God. What God is like is known as we find out what His Son is like: for 'Jesus' read 'Immanuel', 'God-with-us'.

JESUS IS GOD'S FREE AND PERFECT GIFT TO US

As is the way of the world, Rome laid extortionate claim to people's taxes. Everything must be paid for; there's no such thing as a free lunch. Nothing is for nothing. But Jesus is the free gift of God's grace. He does not come with God's tax demand. So many get it wrong at this point, assuming that God is a book-keeping God, obsessed with accounting. They view God as though He relishes getting us into arrears with what we owe Him by our default. But our debt, like that of some Third World countries, is unpayable and has to be written off. And contrary to persistent rumour, His way is not a list of 'do's', 'don'ts' and demands.

The fact is that the book-keeping God exists only as a figment of our self-righteous imagination. Any such books have been shredded and incinerated long ago in the fire of His free forgiveness and love. There is no debt to pay; it's been cancelled. Which is why living with Him is not a crushing burden. The Christian message – the message of Christmas and Easter – is not about the sacrifice *we* make, but the sacrifice *He* makes – and in which we trust. It's about His tax-free gift of salvation in Jesus Christ. Jesus embodies God's own self-giving, the giving of Himself for our salvation: Immanuel, God's very own life given to us freely, without charge to our account. Jesus is God's perfect gift.

JESUS IS THE FOCUS OF GOD'S GLORY

To engage with God's glory is not a matter of seeing supernatural lights on a hillside nor of witnessing strange angelic appearances, experiences exclusive to those fortunate enough to be in the right place at the right time. As Lewis Smedes wisely reminds us:

> To experience the glory of God is to experience God's excellence, his splendid essence; it is to know the secret of what God is really like. Where do we experience the glory of God? We see hints of his glory in the trembling hosts of heaven, no doubt. We hear rumours of his glory in a thousand symphonies. But if you want to experience what God is really like, if you want to know his glory, you see it in the face of a man – his name is Jesus.[2]

The face of Jesus is the face of *this* God turned towards us in grace. In His birth He is God-*with-us*; in His death the God who is with us is the God who is *for us*; in His resurrection and post-ascension donation He is the God with us and *in us* by the Spirit.

Jesus is the incarnate excellence of God. Jesus is the best God can be and do. Jesus is God's perfect gift. The face of the healer is the face of God with us! The face of the man on the cross is the face of God with us! And so it is that the glory of this baby is the glory of Christ, the image of God. The whole gospel can be summed up as 'having the face of Christ shining in our hearts'.[3]

'For God, who said, "Let light shine out of darkness," made his light shine in our hearts to give us the light of the knowledge of the glory of God in the face of Christ' (2 Cor. 4:6; cf. John 1:14–18)

JESUS IS THE FINAL TRUTH AND WISDOM OF GOD

As we said earlier, the lesson of the Magi is that true wisdom is found neither in the East nor in the West, but in Jesus Christ 'in whom are hidden all the treasures of wisdom and knowledge'. Our postmodern, web-sited, Internet world is awash with wisdom. But as T.S. Eliot observed half a century ago: 'Where is the wisdom we have lost in knowledge?' Information is the name of our contemporary game. The information superhighway is Route One for today's idle and curious. We teach IT (information technology) in our schools. But wisdom is not IT but a Person, Jesus Christ: the living, dying and risen embodiment of the God Who is with us.

JESUS IS THE SIGN OF GOD'S EXTRAORDINARY HUMILITY

Christmas turns its back on Roman power and splendour, Roman prestige and self-aggrandisement – the representative panoply of worldly pomp and circumstance – in favour of what can be called only the amazing humility of God. In Christ, God stoops to conquer us in the same manner as He would stoop to wash the feet of a dirty world. He condescends to our level of frail humanity, risking all to get close up to us. *This* is the God Who is with us in Jesus, a God Who is vulnerable and open to rejection, a God Who in the Person of His Son suffers on a cross in ways beyond our understanding.

All this is good news for those today who, like Joseph and Mary, are burdened down with impossible dreams, weighed down with making a living and meeting the Inland Revenue's demands, finding and keeping a roof over their head, bringing up children as best they can in a dangerous and uncertain world. The mundane journey that is our everyday existence might just be about to collide with the eternal and transcendent purposes of the living God, the God Who loves us enough to give us His Son.

Like the shepherds we may not, up to this point, have given much thought to these matters. Life is short and busy; but just for a moment we are perhaps stopped in our tracks, surprised by a sudden joy, intrigued by a glimpse of glory, gripped by a Voice. If so we can start out on a personal journey to Bethlehem now; by making the move that brings us to

Jesus the Infant Who, being God, invites our worship. Come and believe with the believing that is seeing. Get a life, a new life from God. Catch the true spirit of Christmas, which is not a passing, frivolous moment, but an everlasting joy. Receive the perfect gift.

POSTSCRIPT

The Real Thing

> That which was from the beginning, which we have heard, which we have seen with our eyes, which we have looked at and our hands have touched – this we proclaim concerning the Word of life. The life appeared; we have seen it and testify to it, and we proclaim to you the eternal life, which was with the Father and has appeared to us. We proclaim to you what we have seen and heard, so that you also may have fellowship with us. And our fellowship is with the Father and with his Son, Jesus Christ. We write this to make our joy complete.
>
> 1 John 1:1–4

As I read these words at a two-thousand-year distance, it is as though I can feel the catch in the throat and the wide-eyed wonder of the aged apostle who has never got over the staggering, mind-blowing miracle of the incarnation. 'I was there' – 'I was there when it happened, I can speak with first-hand testimony, I saw and heard and handled with my own hands the very "word of life".' John has simply never got over it!

We have a deep, in-built hunger for reality. All our senses are attuned to it. Of course, we all know we settle too easily for substitutes, a placebo of existence for the real thing. But still we strain our ears to catch the echo of a music we have never heard. We long to hear a voice from beyond ourselves. And for a split second we think we hear it in a lover's whisper, a child's laughter, or when a poem tugs at our heartstrings. We listen to exalted music in eager hope of hearing it ... and the choirs, melodies, ethereal harmonies and swelling sounds persuade us that we are eavesdropping on the original concern of all joy and truth.

We want to see; we long to see with our own eyes the final evidence that life is really worth living. We grow tired of invisible gods and spirits, and yearn for one glimmer of light that would persuade us that God exists. We gaze on nature's beauty, feast our sight on majestic mountains and sun-kissed landscapes, peering into the wonder to glimpse that glory and momentarily, as sunlight dapples water, we can convince ourselves that we caught sight of a burning bush.

Above all, our deeply ingrained suspicion – fuelled by modern scientific materialism – doubts any reality we cannot touch and handle. We want the authentic to be made audible, reality to be made visible, truth to be tangible.

All, this and more John declares he has found in the unique and wondrous Person of Jesus of Nazareth. No wonder the aged John could never get over it!

MANIFESTATION

The very 'logos of life' – that which is the very meaning of life itself, the very reason that pulsates behind all living things, the very beating heart of the whole universe, the ultimate reason for living of everything that exists – all this John has met in person.

This Life appeared, was manifest and John has heard it, seen it, touched it. No wonder John could never get over it!

This is what scholars call the 'scandal of particularity' – the extraordinary, even offensive, fact that universal truth, the living pulse behind all that exists, in all the ages, is concentrated here in this one brief human life, at this one particular time in the long ages of history, at this one spot on the earth's surface.

John and his fellow-apostles have heard Him speak His parables, watched Him as He welcomed children and touched lepers, slept beside Him under hedges on summer nights, sat beside Him at dinner, seen Him die with arms outstretched in agony on a cross, met Him risen from the dead again in wondering adoration and gazed upon His scars. Fishermen, artisans, disciples of Jesus had seen and known. No wonder John couldn't get over it! 'The secret of the universe stood unveiled before his eyes.'[1]

This one Jew in first-century Palestine is the key to it all – the One in and through Whom the ultimate reality of God and the world, of relationships and living, of past, present and future is uniquely and finally disclosed. And John has been telling everyone about it ever since.

'That which was from the beginning' (1 John 1:1) is what John proclaims. The curiously impersonal pronouns 'what' or 'that which' conceal rather than diminish the personal achievement at the heart of the story. Since, as R.E. Brown argues, neuter pronouns can function 'comprehensively to cover the person, words, and works', Gary Burge concludes that the words '"what" or "that which" are shorthand for "the whole career of Jesus"'.[2]

The words 'from the beginning' therefore probably mean 'from the beginning of Jesus' life and ministry' though, bearing in mind how John 1 opens with its conscious echo of Genesis 1 ('In the beginning was the Word …' / 'In the beginning God …'), John may well have left it deliberately ambiguous as to whether he is referring to the start of Jesus' human journey or to His eternal origins.

The statement: 'this we proclaim concerning the Word of life' is rich and gathers in many strands of truth.

- 'Logos' ('Word') – in the Old Testament and Jewish tradition – is the creative self-expression of God.
- 'Logos' – in the Greek thinkers – is the coherent reason or meaning behind the life of the universe.
- 'Logos' – for the apostles – is the message of and about Jesus Christ, the Word of God made flesh, Who dwelt among us so that we beheld His glory.

This is the Life that appeared – this verifiable human life – which was at the same time the very life of the One Creator God; this historic life in the flesh was at the same time the manifestation of that 'eternal life, which was with the Father …'.

Now this is the hard part; what happened to John is *not* going to happen to us! What happened to John – what he heard and saw and touched – happened then and happened once. It was unique and unrepeatable.

We have to believe on the strength of his word; we have to trust his testimony; we have to take to heart and risk everything on his proclamation being true. Our faith is historically grounded and based, and there is no way round that. But history is a place where we all have to be. For nothing can undo what has surely happened. History is, of course, a scary place to be. This is a burden sometimes; we have sad memories, sometimes bad memories of what has happened to us or been done to us and we want the past healed rather than honoured. But history can also be a safe place.

Frederick Buechner has a wonderful piece in which he celebrates the joys of being alive. In the course of it he writes of those historic moments of awareness and aliveness – that 'having-beenness' – from which nothing can ever separate us: like that one day, out of so many, he met his children out of school.

> I pick the children up at the bottom of the mountain where the orange bus lets them off in the wind. They run for the car like leaves blowing. Not for keeps, to be sure, but at least for the time being, the world has given them back again, and whatever the world chooses to do later on, it can never so much as lay a hand on the having-beenness of this time. The past is inviolate. We are none of us safe, but everything that has happened is safe. In all the vast and empty reaches of the universe it can never be otherwise that when the orange bus stopped with its red lights blinking, these two children were on it. Their noses were running. One of them dropped a sweater. I drove them home.[3]

PROCLAMATION AND PARTICIPATION

John's proclamation is with a view to our participation in the same reality he enjoys: 'we proclaim to you what we have seen and heard, so that you also may have fellowship with us' (1 John 1:3). Our participation in the reality of the Word of life that is the eternal life of God, though different from John's, is no less real. If we ask how such a definite, unique and historic experience is transmitted and shared across the generations, then the answer is – by John's proclamation.

As we hear and receive John's testimony, as we believe his message and embrace his gospel, then genuine connections are made. We have 'fellowship' with John and the first apostles and – more importantly – through their testimony, we have fellowship with Father and with His Son Jesus Christ.

There are in fact three strands to the way we experience the Word of life for ourselves.

- We receive and believe what John proclaims, his first-hand testimony to the truth made visible and tangible among us. In other words, we can have no authentic experience of or relationship with God without this being anchored in the apostolic gospel, without this being rooted in the truth of what the first apostles heard, saw, handled and told of Who Jesus really was.
- But at the same time, through faith in this gospel and by adhering to it, we ourselves can enjoy a real, experiential relationship with the living God as our Father and with Jesus as His Son. Believing the

gospel is no mere cerebral assent to doctrines but a wholehearted embrace by faith of the message, which ushers us into the realms of real spiritual experience and relationship.

- Furthermore, this experience of God is not a lonely isolated or solitary one, even though it is personal and individual. Our fellowship with the Father and the Son is enjoyed in concert with other believers – indeed with believers from across the ages.

This clearly sets the stage for all that John wants to say. Christian spiritual experience is a blend of historic facts, propositional truth, spiritual experience and relational fellowship, and these are to be held together. Evangelical Christianity has sometimes reacted to the threat from a vague and ill-defined liberalism by downplaying the role of experience in favour of propositional truth, with the result that we have lopsided rather than holistic Christians. Equally a charismatic type of Christianity is in danger of majoring on spiritual experiences that disdain doctrine and lose touch with the revelation of the humanity of Jesus spelt out by the apostles in the New Testament.

John will have none of this, as we shall see. He starts with personal disclosures in history – what he has personally witnessed. But he shows how this issues in a clear proclamation to others outside that original group and to later generations. When they receive it as gospel and believe it, they can go through an open door to enter into an experience of this God and His Son, Whom they are asked to confess and profess with unswerving conviction and Whom they are to imitate in their life and behaviour. See how wonderfully rounded and integrated a view of the Christian life John has.

EXHILARATION

'This completes our joy' (see 1 John 1:4). Remarkable connections are set up between what was seen and heard from the beginning, what was proclaimed, and the ensuing fellowship with God, which is a fellowship with all other believers. This completes the vital circuit of joy!

Martyn Lloyd-Jones discusses the heart of joy, describing it as:

- 'satisfaction' – an integration of intellectual, emotional, volitional desires being satisfied;
- 'a spirit of exultation' – that flush of feeling, an active, exultant note;
- a 'feeling of strength and power' that makes us fear nothing, lifts us above ourselves, makes us robust and defiant.

Of course only Jesus had this joy in full and free expression, so only He can give it and only in fellowship with the Father and with others is it sustained.[4]

This is John's proclamation (Greek *appangellomen*, 'we proclaim'). John is an 'angelos' in declaring this; not a lecturer, not a speculator, not a suggester or a sharer, but an announcer, a proclaimer.

The only reason why Christians are here today is that in one place and time certain things happened that cannot be undone, a certain life appeared. It blazed like a comet across our night sky and was gone but it has left an unmistakable and unforgettable afterglow. John was there; he bathed in the light. He heard and saw and touched, and now proclaims for all time that this is the very Word of life, the Truth beyond all truths, the Reality beyond all reality.

Sir Edward Elgar, at the end of the original score of his great oratorio *The Dream of Gerontius* wrote these words:

> This is the best of me: for the rest, I ate, and drank, and slept, and loved and hated, like another; my life was as the vapour, and is not. But this I saw and knew; this if anything of mine, is worth your memory.

Eugene Peterson paraphrased the opening words of John's first epistle like this:

> From the very first day, we were there, taking it all in – we heard it with our own ears, saw it with our own eyes, verified it with our own hands. The Word of Life appeared right before our eyes; we saw it happen! And now we're telling you in most sober prose that what we witnessed was, incredibly, this: The infinite Life of God himself took shape before us.
>
> We saw it, we heard it, and now we're telling you so that you can experience it along with us, this experience of communion with the Father and his Son, Jesus Christ. Our motive for writing is simply this: We want

> you to enjoy this, too. Your joy will double our joy!' (1 John 1:1–4, *The Message*)

In a typically austere poem R.S. Thomas pondered the tear-stained record of history. As time passes, he muses, history 'commits adultery with it to father the cause of its continued weeping'. But alongside this bleak vision of history, the poet has another angle of vision:

> I have seen the sun break through
> to illuminate a small field
> for a while, and gone my way
> and forgotten it. But that was the pearl
> of great price, the one field that had
> the treasure in it. I realise now
> that I must give all that I have
> to possess it. Life is not hurrying
>
> on to a receding future, nor hankering after
> an imagined past. It is the turning
> aside like Moses to the miracle
> of the lit bush, to a brightness
> that seemed as transitory as your youth
> once, but is the eternity that awaits you.[5]

For us, as for apostles and evangelists, and indeed for the Christian poet, R.S. Thomas, incarnation is our burning bush and Jesus our 'bright field' in Whom is hidden all the treasures of God's kingdom. Jesus is God's perfect gift.

NOTES

Preview: Perfect Timing

1. Dylan Thomas, 'Fern Hill' in Walford Davies and Ralph Maud (eds.), *Dylan Thomas: Collected Poems 1934–1953* (London: J.M. Dent and Sons Ltd., 1989), p.135.
2. Jaroslav Pelikan, *Jesus through the Centuries: His Place in the History of Cultures* (New Haven: Yale University Press, 1985), p.32.

Chapter 1 – Great Preparations – Matthew's Viewpoint

1. See Matthew 1:22–23; 2:15, 17, 23; also 4:14ff.; 12:17–21; 13:14–15, 35; 27:9ff.
2. Herman Hendrickx, *The Infancy Narratives* (London: Geoffrey Chapman, 1984), p.23.
3. Frederick Dale Bruner, *Matthew, Volume 1, The Christbook, Matthew 1–12* (Dallas: Word, 1987), p.7.
4. Respectively, Craig Keener, *A Commentary on Matthew* (Grand Rapids: Eerdmans, 1999), pp.76–77; and Beverley Roberts Gaventa, *Mary, Glimpses of the Mother of Jesus* (Edinburgh: T. & T. Clark, 1992), p.38.
5. Bruner, *Matthew 1–12*, p.1.
6. Ibid., p.67.
7. See James M. Scott, '"For as many as are of works of the Law are under a curse" (Galatians 3:10)' in Craig A. Evans and James A. Sanders (eds.), *Paul and the Scriptures of Israel* (Sheffield: JSOT, Sheffield Academic Press, 1993), pp.187–221; and 'Restoration of Israel' in Gerald F. Hawthorne, Ralph P. Martin and Daniel G. Reid (eds.), *Dictionary of Paul and His Letters* (Downers Grove: InterVarsity Press, 1993), pp.796–805.

Chapter 2 – Great Expectations – Luke's Story

1. James S. Stewart, *The Gates of New Life* (Edinburgh: T. & T. Clark, 1941), pp.153–4.
2. N.T. Wright, *The New Testament and the People of God* (London: SPCK, 1992), p.379.
3. Luke Timothy Johnson, *The Gospel of Luke: Sacra Pagina Series* (Collegeville: The Liturgical Press, 1991), pp.34–35.
4. Wright, *New Testament*, p.380.

5. Ibid.
6. See Ezekiel 3:26–27; Daniel 10:15–17.
7. Wright, *New Testament*, p.381.

Chapter 5 – East-Side Story

1. Ben Witherington III, *Women in the Earliest Churches* (Cambridge: Cambridge University Press, 1988), p.134.
2. Ibid.
3. R.E. Brown, *The Birth of the Messiah* (London: Geoffrey Chapman, 1993), p.333.
4. Elaine Storkey, *Mary's Story, Mary's Song* (London: Harper Collins, 1993), p.52.
5. Ibid.
6. Hendrickx, *Infancy Narratives*, p.72.

Chapter 6 – The Child and Madonna

1. Austin Farrer, *A Faith of Our Own*, (Cleveland: The World Publishing Company, 1960), p.34.
2. Max Turner, *Power from on High: The Spirit in Israel's Restoration and Witness in Luke–Acts* (Sheffield: Sheffield Academic Press, 1996), p.159.
3. Hendrickx, *Infancy Narratives*, p.125.
4. Joel B. Green, *The Theology of Luke* (Cambridge: Cambridge University Press, 1995), p.143
5. Storkey, *Mary's Story*, p.17.
6. R.T. France, 'Mary's Song; The Magnificat' in David Wright (ed.), *Chosen by God: Mary in Evangelical Perspective* (London: Marshall Pickering, 1989), p.41.
7. Wright, *Chosen by God*, p.8.
8. Ibid., p.42.
9. Green, *Theology of Luke*, p.142.

Chapter 7 – Minding God's Own Business

1. Austin Farrer, *The Brink of Mystery* (London: SPCK, 1976), p.21.
2. Dietrich Bonhoeffer, *Letters and Papers from Prison* (London: Collins, 1963), p.122.
3. Austin Farrer, *A Celebration of Faith* (London: Hodder and Stoughton, 1970), p.104.
4. Austin Farrer, *The End of Man* (London: SPCK,1973), p.58.

Chapter 8 – The Aerial View

1. J.B. Phillips, *New Testament Christianity* (London: Hodder and Stoughton, 1956), pp.27–33.
2. See the stirring work of John Piper, especially *Desiring God: Meditations of a Christian Hedonist* (Portland: Multnomah, 1986).

Chapter 9 – Glory in the Night

1. Joel B. Green, *The Gospel of Luke: New International Commentary on the New Testament* (Grand Rapids: Eerdmans, 1997), p.127.
2. Ibid., p.132.
3. Ibid., p.133.
4. Hendrickx, *Infancy Narratives*, p.96.
5. Helmut Thielicke, *The Silence of God* (Grand Rapids: Eerdmans, 1962), p.63.

Chapter 10 – The Messianic Secret

1. Farrer, *Celebration of Faith*, p.204.
2. Martyn Lloyd-Jones, *God's Ultimate Purpose: An Exposition of Ephesians One* (Edinburgh: Banner of Truth Trust, 1978), pp.131–132.
3. Emil Brunner, *The Mediator* (London: Lutterworth Press, 1963), p.408.
4. P.T. Forsyth, *God the Holy Father* (London: Independent Press, reprinted 1957), p.38.
5. Robert Barron, *And Now I See: A Theology of Imagination* (New York: The Crossroad Publishing Company, 1998), p.199.
6. Farrer, *Faith of Our Own*, p.43.

Chapter 11 – First Family

1. Jonathan Sacks, *The Politics of Hope* (London: Jonathan Cape, 1997), pp.185ff.
2. Rodney Clapp, *Families at the Crossroads: Beyond Traditional and Modern Options* (Downers Grove; IVP, 1993), p.79.
3. For this lovely phrase see Thomas Howard, *Once Upon a Time, God …* (London: Lakeland, 1974), p.60.

4. Calvin Miller, *The Singer* (London: Falcon, 1976), pp.34–35, 44–45. This beautiful allegory is still in print in more recent editions.

Chapter 12 – A Spirit-Stirred Man

1. Green, *Gospel of Luke*, p.145.
2. Hendrickx, *Infancy Narratives*, p.107.
3. Martyn Lloyd-Jones, *Expository Sermons on 2 Peter* (Edinburgh: Banner of Truth Trust, 1983), p.194.
4. Green, *Gospel of Luke*, p.146.
5. Ibid.
6. Hendrickx, *Infancy Narratives*, p.109.
7. Titled song, 'Now that I've held him in my arms', from the album *Legacy* (Milk and Honey Records, 1983).

Chapter 13 – Prophetic Sign, Painful Sword

1. John Morrish in a British national newspaper, *The Daily Telegraph*.
2. Ibid.
3. E.M.B. Green, *The Meaning of Salvation* (Hodder and Stoughton, 1965), p.72.
4. John Nolland, *Luke: Word Biblical Commentary* (Dallas: Word), p.125.

Chapter 14 – His Majesty the Baby

1. Earl Jabay, *The Kingdom of Self* (Plainfield, New Jersey: Logos), pp.7–8.
2. Richard A. Horsley, *The Liberation of Christmas: The Infancy Narratives in Social Context* (New York: Crossroad, 1989), p.44.
3. Ben Witherington III, *The Jesus Quest* (Carlisle: Paternoster, 1995), p.16.
4. J.R.R. Tolkein, *The Lord of the Rings* (London: George Allen and Unwin, 1969), p.988.
5. G.K. Chesterton, 'The House of Christmas' in *The Spirit of Christmas* (London: Xanadu, 1984), p.35.
6. Donald A. Hagner, *Matthew 1–13: Word Biblical Commentary* (Dallas: Word, 1993), p.42.
7. Bruner, *Matthew: Volume 1*, p.44.

8. Ibid., p.45.
9. D.A. Carson, 'Matthew' in Frank E. Gaebelein (ed.) *The Expositor's Bible Commentary: Volume 8* (Grand Rapids: Zondervan, 1984), p.95.

Chapter 15 – Ready-Made or Self-Assembly?

1. Oswald Chambers, *The Psychology of Redemption* (London: Marshall, Morgan & Scott, reprt. 1955), p.39.
2. Farrer, *Celebration of Faith*, p.89.
3. Daniel Taylor, *Letters to My Children* (Downers Grove: IVP, 1989), pp.163, 123–124, 155–158.

Chapter 16 – The Journey

1. Frederick Buechner, *The Magnificent Defeat* (San Francisco: Harper and Row, 1966), pp.70–71.
2. Lewis B. Smedes, *How Can It Be All Right When Everything Is All Wrong?* (San Francisco: Harper, 1992), p.88.
3. David F. Ford, *The Shape of Living* (Grand Rapids: Baker, 1997), p.47.

Postscript: The Real Thing

1. G.C. Findlay, *Fellowship in the Life Eternal: Expositions of 1 John* (London: Hodder and Stoughton, 1909), p.85.
2. Raymond E. Brown, *The Epistles of John, The Anchor Bible* (London: Geoffrey Chapman, 1983), p.154; Gary M. Burge, *Letters of John: The NIV Application Commentary* (Grand Rapids: Zondervan, 1996), p.53.
3. Frederick Buechner, *The Alphabet of Grace* (New York: Harper and Row, 1979), p.110.
4. I cannot trace this reference, p.210
5. R.S. Thomas, 'The Bright Field' in *Later Poems: 1972–1982* (London; Pan Macmillan, 1983), p.81.

NATIONAL DISTRIBUTORS

UK: (and countries not listed below)
CWR, Waverley Abbey House, Waverley Lane, Farnham, Surrey GU9 8EP.
Tel: (01252) 784710 Outside UK (44) 1252 784710

AUSTRALIA: CMC Australasia, PO Box 519, Belmont, Victoria 3216.
Tel: (03) 5241 3288

CANADA: CMC Distribution Ltd, PO Box 7000, Niagara on the Lake, Ontario L0S 1J0.
Tel: 1800 325 1297

GHANA: Challenge Enterprises of Ghana, PO Box 5723, Accra.
Tel: (021) 222437/223249 Fax: (021) 226227

HONG KONG: Cross Communications Ltd, 1/F, 562A Nathan Road, Kowloon.
Tel: 2780 1188 Fax: 2770 6229

INDIA: Crystal Communications, 10-3-18/4/1, East Marredpally, Secunderabad – 500 026.
Tel/Fax: (040) 7732801

KENYA: Keswick Bookshop, PO Box 10242, Nairobi.
Tel: (02) 331692/226047 Fax: (02) 728557

MALAYSIA: Salvation Book Centre (M) Sdn Bhd, 23 Jalan SS 2/64,
47300 Petaling Jaya, Selangor.
Tel: (03) 78766411/78766797 Fax: (03) 78757066/78756360

NEW ZEALAND: CMC Australasia, PO Box 36015, Lower Hutt.
Tel: 0800 449 408 Fax: 0800 449 049

NIGERIA: FBFM, Helen Baugh House, 96 St Finbarr's College Road, Akoka, Lagos.
Tel: (01) 7747429/4700218/825775/827264

PHILIPPINES: OMF Literature Inc, 776 Boni Avenue, Mandaluyong City.
Tel: (02) 531 2183 Fax: (02) 531 1960

REPUBLIC OF IRELAND: Scripture Union, 40 Talbot Street, Dublin 1.
Tel: (01) 8363764

SINGAPORE: Armour Publishing Pte Ltd, Block 203A Henderson Road,
11–06 Henderson Industrial Park, Singapore 159546.
Tel: 276 9976 Fax: 276 7564

SOUTH AFRICA: Struik Christian Books, 80 MacKenzie Street,
PO Box 1144, Cape Town 8000.
Tel: (021) 462 4360 Fax: (021) 461 3612

SRI LANKA: Christombu Books, 27 Hospital Street, Colombo 1.
Tel: (01) 433142/328909

TANZANIA: CLC Christian Book Centre, PO Box 1384, Mkwepu Street, Dar es Salaam.
Tel/Fax (022) 2119439

USA: CMC Distribution, PO Box 644, Lewiston, New York, 14092-0644.
Tel: 1800 325 1297

ZIMBABWE: Word of Life Books, Shop 4, Memorial Building,
35 S Machel Avenue, Harare.
Tel: (04) 781305 Fax: (04) 774739

For email addresses, visit the CWR website: www.cwr.org.uk

God's Story

God's Story is the third key title in the popular *Cover to Cover* series.

This exciting and beautifully illustrated annual reading programme reveals Scripture as an epic story, taking you through the Bible promise by promise. See how God reveals Himself through His covenant encounters with His people and share in God's great narrative as it unfolds through biblical history. Each daily reading brings you closer to an understanding of the relationship between the Old and New Testaments, helping you to discover your true identity as part of the New Creation in Christ.

God's Story softback book
ISBN 1-85345-186-X

Every Day with Jesus

With over half-a-million readers, *Every Day with Jesus* is one of the most popular daily devotionals in the world. Get practical help with life's challenges and gain a deeper insight into essential biblical truths.

First Steps in Faith

Every Day with Jesus for People in Search of God is a great tool for friendship evangelism, answering all those demanding questions that people often struggle with, by providing clear, thoughtful answers. Selwyn Hughes offers an intelligent perspective on life's big issues, including:

ISBN 1-85345-226-2

- What is life all about?
- Is there life after death?
- Who is God and what is He like?
- How can I know God?
- Why does God allow suffering?

Every Day with Jesus for new Christians is a powerful and relevant guide for people new to the Christian faith. A favourite with churches of all denominations, with over half-a-million copies in print.

ISBN 1-85345-133-9

Bible Study Guides for Today's Church

New Bible studies from the *Cover to Cover* series, created to provide a unique resource for group and individual study lasting between one and two hours. Seven stimulating sessions in each book, supported by opening ice-breakers, Bible references, discussion starters and suggestions for personal application.

The Image of God
His Attributes and Character
ISBN 1-85345-228-9

The Tabernacle
Entering into God's Presence
ISBN 1-85345-230-0

The Uniqueness of our Faith
What makes Christianity Distinctive?
ISBN 1-85345-232-7

Ruth
Loving Kindness in Action
ISBN 1-85345-231-9

Mark
Life as it is Meant to be Lived
ISBN 1-85345-233-5

Ephesians
Claiming your Inheritance
ISBN 1-85345-229-7

Great Ways to Share Your Faith

This new series from Selwyn Hughes offers intelligent, honest perspectives on life, faith and God for those in search of answers to the big questions. A wonderful resource for friendship evangelism that will encourage anyone searching for God.

Can I Really Know God?

ISBN 1-85345-234-3

- Is God there?
- Can I have a relationship with God?
- What can I do to really know God?

Can I Really Know Fulfilment?

ISBN 1-85345-235-1

- Is happiness really possible?
- Why won't the pain go away?
- Doesn't death end it all?
- What is the answer?

Bible Classics

An attractive and easy-to-read series exploring God's will for our lives, making us the people He called us to be. These make wonderful gifts for friends and family. Based on popular editions of *Every Day with Jesus.*

The Lord's Prayer
ISBN 1-85345-193-2

The 23rd Psalm
ISBN 1-85345-192-4

The Divine Eagle
ISBN 1-85345-190-8

The Divine Gardener
ISBN 1-85345-191-6